Coaching YMCA Rookies Basketball

YOUTH SUPER SPORTS
We build strong kids, strong families, strong communities.

Library of Congress Cataloging-in-Publication Data

Coaching YMCA Rookies basketball / YMCA of the USA.
    p. cm.
    Includes bibliographical references (p.) and index.
    ISBN 0-7360-0337-1
    1. Basketball for children--Coaching.   I. YMCA of the USA.
  GV886.25.C63   1999
  796.323'07'7--dc21   99-15054
   CIP

ISBN: 0-7360-0337-1

Published for the YMCA of the USA by Human Kinetics Publishers, Inc. Item no.: Y5487
Copyright © 1999 National Council of Young Men's Christian Associations of the United States of America

Material in chapter 9 and on pages 22–24 and 145–148 is adapted, by permission, from American Sport Education Program, 1996, *Coaching Youth Basketball,* 2d ed. (Champaign, IL: Human Kinetics). Material on pages 142–144 is adapted, by permission, from R. Martens, 1997, *Successful Coaching,* Updated 2d ed. (Champaign, IL: Human Kinetics). Material on pages 148–155 is adapted, by permission, from M.J. Flegel, 1997, *Sport First Aid,* Updated ed. (Champaign, IL: Human Kinetics).

All rights reserved. Except for use in a review, the reproduction or utilization of this work in any form or by any electronic, mechanical, or other means, now known or hereafter invented, including xerography, photocopying, and recording, and in any information storage and retrieval system, is forbidden without the written permission of the publisher.

YMCA Project Coordinator: Richard Jones
YMCA Curriculum Consultant: Linda Griffin
Content Consultant: Karen Partlow
Fitness and Character Development Consultant: Kathleen Madden
Project Writer: Patricia Sammann
Managing Editor: Coree Schutter
Assistant Editors: Chris Enstrom, Sandra Merz Bott, and John Wentworth
Copyeditor: Heather Stith
Proofreader: Erin Cler
Graphic Designer: Robert Reuther
Graphic Artist: Tara Welsch
Photo Editor: Clark Brooks
Cover Designer: Jack W. Davis
Photographer (cover and interior): Tom Roberts
Illustrators: Mic Greenberg and Sharon Smith (Mac art), Roberto Sabas (line drawings), Dick Flood and Timothy Stiles (cartoons)
Printer: United Graphics

Printed in the United States of America   10 9 8 7 6 5 4 3 2 1

Copies of this book may be purchased from the YMCA Program Store P.O. Box 5076, Champaign, IL 61825-5076, (800) 747-0089.

The YMCA of the USA does not operate or manage the YMCA Youth Super Sports program or any of its components or facilities associated with the program.

Contents

Part I   The Job 1

Chapter 1   **Welcome to YMCA Youth Super Sports** 3
- YMCA Youth Super Sports 4
- The YMCA Philosophy of Youth Sports 5
- YMCA Rookies 6
- YMCA Winners 6
- YMCA Champions 7

Chapter 2   **Your Job Description** 9
- Your Duties As a Coach 9
- Being a Good Coach 10

Chapter 3   **Remember They're Kids** 13
- Four- to Five-Year-Olds 13
  - *Physical Characteristics*   13
  - *Social Characteristics*   14
  - *Emotional Characteristics*   15
  - *Cognitive Characteristics*   15
- Six- to Seven-Year-Olds 16
  - *Physical Characteristics*   16
  - *Social Characteristics*   17
  - *Emotional Characteristics*   17
  - *Cognitive Characteristics*   18

Chapter 4   **The Games Approach to Teaching Basketball** 19
- Step 1. Play a Modified Basketball Game 21
- Step 2. Help Players Discover What They Need to Do 21
- Step 3. Teach the Skills of the Game 22
  - *Introduce the Skill*   23
  - *Demonstrate the Skill*   23
  - *Explain the Skill*   24
  - *Attend to Players Practicing the Skill*   24
- Step 4. Practice the Skills in Another Game 24

Contents

Part II The Coaching Plans 27

Chapter 5 The Season Plans 29
  Basketball Curriculum for Four- and Five-Year-Olds 30
  Basketball Curriculum for Six- and Seven-Year-Olds 30

Chapter 6 Practice Plans for Four- to Five-Year-Olds ... 33
  Game Modifications 33
  Practice Plan Organization 36

Chapter 7 Practice Plans for Six- to Seven-Year-Olds ... 75
  Game Modifications 75
  Practice Plan Organization 78

Part III The Building Blocks 113

Chapter 8 Teaching Basketball Skills and Tactics 115
  Position and Movement 115
    The Jump Stop 116
    Pivots, Cuts, and Slides 116
    Triple Threat Position 118
  Ballhandling Skills 119
    Passing 119
    Receiving 121
    Dribbling 121
    Dribbling Dos and Don'ts 122
    Shooting 122
  Defensive Skills 126
    Moving the Feet 126
    Guarding an Opponent With the Ball 126
    Guarding an Opponent Away From the Ball 127
    Rebounding 130

Chapter 9 Teaching Basketball Rules and Traditions .. 131
  Ball and Court Characteristics 131
  Player Equipment 133
  Player Positions 133
  Starting and Restarting the Game 134
  Fouls 134
    Types of Fouls 134
    Consequences of Fouls 135
    Communicating After Fouls 136
  Violations 136
    Types of Violations 136
    Communicating After Violations 136
  Scoring 137
  Officiating Signals 137
  Basketball Traditions 137

Chapter 10 Teaching Fitness and Safety 141

Components of Fitness 142
- *Cardiorespiratory Fitness 142*
- *Muscular Strength and Endurance 142*
- *Flexibility 143*

Training Principles 143
- *Warm-Up/Cool-Down Principle 143*
- *Overload Principle 144*
- *Reversibility Principle 144*
- *Specificity Principle 144*

Healthy Habits 145
- *General Fitness 145*
- *Good Nutrition 145*

Safety Precautions 145
- *Preseason Physical Examination 146*
- *Regular Inspection of Equipment and Facilities 147*
- *Matching Athletes by Maturity 147*
- *Informing Players and Parents of Inherent Risks 147*
- *Proper Supervision and Record Keeping 147*
- *Environmental Conditions 148*

Emergency Care 151
- *Being Prepared 151*
- *Providing First Aid 153*

Legal Liability 155

Chapter 11 Teaching Character Development 157

Being a Good Role Model 158
Understanding Children's Moral Reasoning 159
Using Teachable Moments 160
Using Values Activities 161

Appendix A Finding More Information 163

Books 163
Videos 163
Organizations 164

Appendix B Preparticipation Screening for YMCA Youth Sports Programs 165

Appendix C Emergency Information Card 167

Appendix D Emergency Response Card 168

Appendix E Injury Report 169

Resources and Suggested Readings 170

Part I

The Job

Thank you for agreeing to be a coach in the YMCA Rookies program of YMCA Youth Super Sports. The job is challenging, but with effort and enthusiasm, you'll find it very rewarding. In part I, we'll tell you more about YMCA Youth Super Sports, the best sports program in America.

As we share with you our philosophy about children's sports programs in chapter 1, you'll see why we think YMCA Youth Super Sports is special. In chapter 2, we'll present you with your job description and request that you bring the YMCA philosophy to life as you teach basketball to your young players. Then in chapter 3, we'll give you some idea of what it is like to be a four- to seven-year-old child (in case you've forgotten). This chapter will give you a feel for what your players are capable of understanding and doing.

In chapter 4, we describe the way we want you to teach basketball to your players; we call it the *games approach*. It's not the traditional way adults have taught sports to children, but you'll see why this YMCA way is a better way. It's essential that you understand and use the games approach when you teach YMCA Rookies basketball.

Our overall objectives in part I are to prepare you to do your job well and to impress on you the potential influence you can have on the young people you coach. It's your chance to make a difference!

chapter 1

Welcome to YMCA Youth Super Sports

Thank you for agreeing to be a coach in the YMCA Youth Super Sports program. As a YMCA Rookies coach, you will introduce a group of young people to the game of basketball. We ask you to not only teach them the basic skills and rules of the game, but also make learning the game a joyful experience. You see, we want them to play basketball not only this season, but for many years to come. And we want you to have fun teaching basketball because we'd like you to help us again next season.

In this guide, you'll find essential information about teaching basketball the YMCA way. In the next section, we'll explain more about the best sports program in America, YMCA Youth Super Sports, and especially, the YMCA Rookies program, of which you'll be a part. Next is your job description for being a YMCA Rookies basketball coach, along with some reminders about how to work with four- to seven-year-olds. Then we'll show you how to teach basketball using the games approach and provide you with a season plan and a complete set of practice plans for four- to five-year-olds and another set for six- to seven-year-olds. In the last part, we'll explain to you how to teach the four main components of the basketball season plan: skills and tactics, rules and traditions, fitness and safety, and character development. And throughout the book, Lucky, the YMCA Youth Super Sports mascot, will help illustrate key points. And we hope by seeing Lucky on these pages, you'll be reminded to keep the fun in your practices and games.

Please read the entire guide carefully and consult it regularly during the season. If your YMCA offers you the opportunity to participate in a YMCA Rookies Basketball Coaches Course, be there. The 3 1/2-hour course will help you use our games approach to teaching basketball.

Let's begin by looking at what YMCA Youth Super Sports is, the YMCA's philosophy of youth sports, and the three parts of YMCA Youth Super Sports: YMCA Rookies, YMCA Winners, and YMCA Champions.

YMCA Youth Super Sports

We've named the program YMCA Youth Super Sports because we're confident it's the best-designed sports program for young people ages 4 to 16 available anywhere. We built the program by combining the knowledge of sport scientists, who've spent their careers studying children's sports, with the practical wisdom of YMCA youth sports directors, who have guided millions of young people through sports programs. Our objective for YMCA Youth Super Sports is to help young people not only become better players, but also become better people. We recognize that not every child can win the contest, but every child can be a winner in YMCA Youth Super Sports. That's why our motto for the program is "Building Winners for Life."

The YMCA triangle, representing spirit, mind, and body, is the inspiration for the YMCA Youth Super Sports triangle shown in figure 1.1. YMCA Youth Super Sports is currently designed for five sports—soccer, baseball and softball, basketball, and volleyball—and consists of three programs:

Figure 1.1 YMCA Youth Super Sports triangle.

YMCA Rookies—A precompetitive, instructional program to teach four- to seven-year-old boys and girls the basic skills and rules of the game.

YMCA Winners—The YMCA's unique, values-based competitive sports program for young people ages 8 to 16.

YMCA Champions—An innovative opportunity for 8- to 16-year-olds to demonstrate personal achievement in and through sports.

All three programs have been carefully crafted to maximize the potential for children to have a positive and beneficial experience under your leadership. We now recognize that sports are not just frivolous games in children's lives; sports have a profound influence on them. Through YMCA Youth Super Sports we want to help young people develop character, not become "characters." We want to help them learn to care about others, to be honest, to show respect, and to be responsible.

Of course, sports don't teach these things to young people automatically. What they do is provide young people with a good opportunity to learn about and develop these values when skillful leadership is provided by volunteer adults such as you.

The YMCA Philosophy of Youth Sports

What we want youth sports to be in the YMCA is stated in our Seven Pillars of YMCA Youth Sports:

◎ **Pillar One—Everyone Plays.** We do not use tryouts to select the best players, nor do we cut kids from YMCA Youth Super Sports. Everyone who registers is assigned to a team. During the season everyone receives equal practice time and plays at least half of every game.

◎ **Pillar Two—Safety First.** Although children may get hurt playing sports, we do all we can to prevent injuries. We've modified each sport to make it safer and more enjoyable to play. We ask you to make sure the equipment and facilities are safe and to teach the sport as we've prescribed so that the skills taught are appropriate for the children's developmental level. We ask you to gradually develop your players' fitness levels so they are conditioned for the sport. We also ask you to constantly supervise your young players so that you can stop any unsafe activities.

◎ **Pillar Three—Fair Play.** Fair play is about more than playing by the rules. It's about you and your players showing respect for all who are involved in YMCA Youth Super Sports. It's about you being a role model of good sportsmanship and guiding your players to do the same. Remember, we're more interested in developing children's character through sports than in developing a few highly skilled players.

◎ **Pillar Four—Positive Competition.** We believe competition is a positive process when the pursuit of victory is kept in the right perspective. The right perspective is when adults make decisions that put the best interests of the children before winning the contest. Learning to compete is important for children, and learning to cooperate in a competitive world is an essential lesson of life. We want to help children learn these lessons through YMCA Youth Super Sports.

◎ **Pillar Five—Family Involvement.** YMCA Youth Super Sports encourages parents to be involved appropriately in their child's participation in our sports programs. In addition to parents being helpful as volunteer coaches, officials, and timekeepers, we encourage them to be at practices and games to support their child's participation. To help parents get involved appropriately, YMCA Youth Super Sports offers parent orientation programs.

◎ **Pillar Six—Sport for All.** YMCA Youth Super Sports is an inclusive sports program. That means that children who differ in various characteristics are to be included rather than excluded from participation. We offer sports programs for children who differ in physical abilities by matching them with children of similar abilities and modifying the sport. We offer programs to all children regardless of their race, gender, religious creed, and ability. We ask our adult leaders to encourage and appreciate the diversity of children in our society and to encourage the children and their parents to do the same.

◎ **Pillar Seven—Sport for Fun.** Sports are naturally fun for most children. They love the challenge of mastering the skills of the game, of playing with their friends, and of competing with their peers. Sometimes when adults become involved in children's sports they over-organize and dominate the activity to the point that it destroys children's enjoyment of the sport. If we take the fun out of sports for our children, we are in danger of the children taking themselves out of sports. Remember, the sports are for the children; let them have fun.

YMCA Rookies

YMCA Rookies is a skill development program that prepares children ages four to seven to participate in YMCA Winners, the competitive sports program, and YMCA Champions, the personal sports achievement program. As a coach in YMCA Rookies, we want you to focus on teaching your players the basics of the game in a precompetitive environment where they can focus on learning the sport, not performing to win.

Too often today children are thrust into competitive sports programs with little instruction on the basics of the sport (both the skills and rules of the game). Perhaps children participate in a few practice sessions, but often they do not obtain sufficient instruction or time to develop basic skills in a precompetitive environment. Then, too, many programs do not sufficiently modify the sport to meet the physical and mental abilities of young children.

The consequence of such an introduction to sports is that children who have had early opportunities for instruction and who are physically more gifted often succeed, while those without these advantages are more likely to fail. We designed YMCA Rookies to address these problems by providing a positive introduction to sports for all children.

To ensure having the highest quality coaches, officials, and sports administrators, YMCA Youth Super Sports offers training and educational resources for all adults involved in YMCA Rookies. The purpose of this training is to emphasize the positive objectives of the program and to de-emphasize the winning-at-all-cost mentality, which leads to so many negative practices in youth sports programs.

The training offered to adults involved in the program is just one aspect that makes YMCA Rookies unique. Another is the modifications we've made to the game of basketball so that children progress through the program in developmentally appropriate ways. Modifying the game increases the likelihood that children will experience success and reduces the risk of injury.

##

YMCA Winners is the values based competitive program in YMCA Youth Super Sports. It's for young people ages 8 to 16, with the competition typically grouped in two- to three-year age ranges. The objectives of YMCA Winners are the same as those for YMCA Rookies: learning the skills of the game, the rules of the sport, the relationship between fitness and health, and character development. However, in YMCA Winners these objectives are achieved as players compete with other players and teams.

 YMCA Champions

YMCA Champions is an innovative award program that encourages and recognizes personal achievement in YMCA sports among young people ages 8 to 16. As shown in table 1.1, for young people to earn an award they must demonstrate their mastery of the sport in four areas, or content domains, and within each sport, they have the opportunity to earn three levels of awards.

The four content domains are the following:

1. **Knowledge.** Participants must show that they understand the rules and traditions of the sport and related fitness and health concepts.
2. **Skill.** Young people must demonstrate their mastery of the physical skills of the sport through game-like skill tests.
3. **Participation.** Young people must participate a certain amount in practices and contests for each of the three levels.
4. **Character.** Participants must demonstrate character development through caring, honesty, respect, and responsibility.

In each sport, participants begin at the Bronze level, the first level of achievement. When they have obtained the Bronze Award in that sport, they can move on to the Silver and Gold levels. Participants can be working on a Bronze Award in one sport, a Silver Award in another sport, and a Gold Award in a third sport. They are encouraged to progress through the levels as rapidly as they wish. After participants have earned a Gold Award, they are eligible to join the YMCA Gold Club. The club is an honorary and service club and provides opportunities for leadership.

TABLE 1.1

The YMCA Champions Program

Levels	CONTENT DOMAINS			
	Knowledge	Skill	Participation	Character
Bronze				
Silver				
Gold				

Coaching YMCA Rookies Basketball

YMCA Champions coaches, who act as mentors for the participants, monitor their progress. YMCA Champions coaches are assisted by Gold Leaders, players 14 years old or older who have earned the Gold Award in that sport. The Gold Leaders come from the YMCA Gold Club. They are trained to assist younger players in their preparation for being tested in the four domains, and they assist the YMCA Champions coaches in conducting the evaluations.

As a YMCA Rookies coach, you will play an important role in encouraging young people to participate in both YMCA Winners and YMCA Champions. That encouragement will come not just by urging them to participate, but by helping them learn the basics of the sport while having fun and building their self-worth.

chapter 2

Your Job Description

Now you know what YMCA Youth Super Sports is and what our philosophy (the Seven Pillars of YMCA Youth Sports) is for conducting this unique sports program. You also know that YMCA Rookies emphasizes teaching children basic basketball skills and rules in a precompetitive environment. We'll ask you to teach your players how to play the game of basketball, but the emphasis will be on teaching, not on competing in contests.

Your Duties As a Coach

You have seven duties as a YMCA Rookies basketball coach:

1. Teach the skills and tactics of basketball to the best of your ability. We want you to teach children the physical skills and tactics to play the sport to the best of their ability. Children value the learning of these skills and tactics, and they respect those who can help them master them. Be a good teacher, but remember that not all children have the same ability to learn. A few have the ability to be outstanding, many have the ability to be competent, and a few have the ability to barely play the sport. We ask that you help them all be the best that they can be.

We'll show you an innovative games approach to teaching and practicing these skills that children thoroughly enjoy. These games are designed to be developmentally appropriate for the children you will be teaching. You'll avoid monotonous drills where children stand in line waiting their turn; instead you'll be keeping everyone active practicing basic skills in game-like conditions. To help you, first we'll provide season plans in chapter 5. In chapter 6, we'll give you practice plans for four- to five-year-olds, and in chapter 7, we'll do the same for six- to seven- year-olds. In chapter 8, we'll review with you how to teach the basic skills and provide you with assistance in detecting and correcting errors.

Coaching YMCA Rookies Basketball

2. **Help your players learn the rules and traditions of basketball.** We ask you to teach your players the rules of basketball as they learn the basic skills through the modified games of the sport. Beyond the rules, we also ask you to teach the basic traditions of the sport. By traditions we mean the proper actions to take to show courtesy and avoid injury—in short, to be a good sport. You'll find the rules and traditions for YMCA Rookies basketball in chapter 9.

3. **Help your players to become fit and to value fitness for a lifetime.** We want you to help your players be fit so they can play basketball safely and successfully. But we also want more. We want you to do so in a way that your players learn to become fit on their own, understand the value of fitness, and enjoy training. Thus, we ask you not to make them do push-ups or run laps for punishment. Make it fun to get fit for basketball and make it fun to play basketball so they'll stay fit for a lifetime. In chapter 10, we'll give you some tips on basic fitness for your players.

4. **Help your players develop character.** Character development is teaching children the core values: caring, honesty, respect, and responsibility. These intangible qualities are no less important to teach than ballhandling or defensive skills. We ask you to teach these values to children by (1) conducting Team Circles, which are built into every practice plan, and (2) demonstrating and encouraging behaviors that express these values at all times. Chapter 11 will give you more suggestions about teaching character development.

5. **Ensure the safety of your players.** You are responsible for supervising every aspect of your players' participation in basketball. Make sure the field is clear of hazardous objects and that the children do not engage in activities that might injure themselves or others. You have not only a legal responsibility, but also a moral one to supervise them closely. See chapter 10 for more on safety.

6. **Help each player develop a positive sense of self-worth.** An essential goal in conducting YMCA Youth Super Sports programs is to help children gain a strong, positive sense of their worth as human beings. For each of us, our most important possession is our self-worth. Please teach our children basketball in a way that helps them grow to respect themselves and others.

7. **Make it fun.** Make learning the game a fantastic experience so that your players will want to continue playing for many years to come.

Being a Good Coach

Just what makes a good basketball coach?

 A person who knows the sport of basketball well. If you're not that familiar with the sport, be sure to attend the YMCA Rookies Basketball Coaches Course and study more about the sport. Refer to the list of useful books and videos in appendix A.

Your Job Description

 A person who wants to teach basketball to young people, who cares. Excellent teachers are motivated, have a positive attitude, and give the time to do the job well.

 A person who understands young people, who possesses empathy. Empathy is caring about the young people you teach by showing you understand them.

We hope you'll do your best to be a good basketball coach for the children on your team. By doing so, you can help them develop their spirits, minds, and bodies, which is the goal for all YMCA programs.

chapter 3

Remember They're Kids

One challenge of working with youngsters is that you need to relate to them as children, not as miniature adults. To do this, you must understand where they're coming from—that is, where they are in their development physically, socially, emotionally, and intellectually. What makes it even more interesting is that on any team you coach, you'll likely find early maturers and late bloomers, and this variance applies not only to your group as a whole, but also to each individual. For example, one player may be intellectually mature and quick to understand basketball tactics and skills, but she may be slow in physical development and thus have difficulty in successfully executing the skills. Another may be developed physically but underdeveloped emotionally.

The more familiar you are with the physical capabilities and mind-sets of children, the better you'll be able to communicate with them and help them grow through their experience in basketball. The following lists detail children's development physically, socially, emotionally, and cognitively. Realize that each child will not conform to all the characteristics at any age; this doesn't mean the child is abnormal. These lists provide a general understanding of children's developmental characteristics. Although we can't take you back to when you were four to seven, we can help you remember what it was like—and help you better understand and relate to children.

 ## Four- to Five-Year-Olds

Physical Characteristics

At Four

- Children's running, jumping, hopping, throwing, and catching become better coordinated.

- Galloping and one-foot skipping begin to appear.
- They can ride a tricycle.

At Five

- Children are three and one-half to three and three-quarter feet tall. They may grow from two to three inches and gain from three to six pounds during the year.
- Girls may be about a year ahead of boys in physiological development.
- Children are beginning to have better body control.
- Their large muscles are better developed than the small muscles that control the fingers and hands.
- Their eye and hand coordination is not yet complete.
- Children are vigorous and noisy, but their activity appears to have a definite direction.
- They tire easily and need plenty of rest.

Social Characteristics

At Four

- Children form their first friendships.
- They are becoming less likely to play alone and more likely to play interactively with others.

At Five

- Children are interested in neighborhood games with other children. They sometimes play games to test their skill.
- They like being with other children, and they seem to get along best in small groups.
- Their interests are largely self-centered.
- Children imitate when they play.
- They get along well in taking turns and they respect other's belongings.
- Children show an interest in home activities.

Development characteristics are adapted from the following:

From Berk, Laura E., *Development Through the Lifespan.* Copyright © 1998 by Allyn & Bacon. Adapted by permission.

From Humphrey, James H., *Sports for Children: A Guide for Adults.* Copyright © 1993 by Charles C Thomas, Publisher, Ltd. Adapted by permission.

Emotional Characteristics

At Four

- Self-conscious emotions (shame, embarrassment, guilt, envy, and pride) become more common.

At Five

- Children seldom show jealousy toward younger siblings.
- Children usually see only one way to do things and one answer to a question.
- They are inclined not to change plans in the middle of an activity; instead, they'd rather begin over.
- They may fear being deprived of their mothers.
- They are learning to get along better, but they still may resort to quarreling and fighting.
- They like to be trusted with errands and enjoy performing simple tasks. They want to please and to do what you expect of them.
- They can better interpret, predict, and influence others' emotional reactions.
- They are beginning to sense right and wrong in terms of specific situations.

Cognitive Characteristics

At Four

- They can generalize remembered information from one situation to another.
- They have a basic understanding of causality in familiar situations.

At Five

- They enjoy copying designs, letters, and numbers and counting objects.
- They are interested in completing tasks.
- Their memory for past events is good.
- They are able to plan activities.
- These children may tend to monopolize table conversation.
- They look at books and pretend to read.
- They like recordings, words, and music that tell stories. They also enjoy stories, dramatic plays, and poems.

- Children of this age can sing simple melodies, beat good rhythms, and recognize simple tunes. They enjoy making up dances to music.
- Their daydreams seem to center around make-believe play.
- They have over 2,000 words in their speaking vocabularies and their pronunciation is usually clear. They can speak in complete sentences and can express their needs well in words.
- Their attention span may have increased up to 20 minutes in some cases.

Six- to Seven-Year-Olds

Physical Characteristics

At Six

- Children are three and one-half to four feet tall and grow gradually.
- They usually have a lot of energy.
- They like to move, doing things such as running, jumping, chasing, and playing dodging games.
- Their muscular control is becoming more effective with large objects.
- A noticeable change occurs in eye-hand behavior. Children can tie their shoes and write their names.
- Children's legs are lengthening rapidly.

At Seven

- They may grow two to three inches and gain three to five pounds during the year.
- They may tire easily and show fatigue in the afternoon.
- Whole-body movements are under better control.
- Children can throw better and catch more accurately.
- Children's reaction times are slow.
- Eye-hand coordination improves.
- Children's hearts and lungs are smallest in proportion to their body size.
- Children may be susceptible to disease and have low resistance.
- Children's endurance is low.
- Small accessory muscles are developing.

Social Characteristics

At Six
- These children are self-centered and need praise.
- They like to be first.
- Sex differences are not of great importance to them at this age.
- They enjoy group play when groups are small.
- Children like parties, but their behavior may not always be proper.
- Most of them like school and have a desire to learn.
- They are interested in the conduct of their friends.
- They show an interest in group approval.

At Seven
- They want recognition for individual achievements.
- They are not always good losers.
- They often talk about their families.
- They are interested in friends and are not influenced by friends' social or economic status.
- They begin to learn to stand up for their rights.
- Some children may have nervous habits, such as nail biting, tongue sucking, scratching, or pulling on the ear.
- Children are beginning to have a sense of time.
- Children show signs of being cooperative.

Emotional Characteristics

At Six
- Their anger may be difficult to control at times.
- Their behavior may often be explosive and unpredictable.
- Sometimes children show jealousy toward siblings, but at other times the children take pride in them.
- They are greatly excited by anything new.
- They may be self-assertive and dramatic.

At Seven
- They have learned more control over anger.
- They become less impulsive and boisterous than at six.

- Their curiosity and creative desires may condition their responses.
- Children are critical of themselves and sensitive to failure. It may be difficult for them to take criticism from adults, and they are overanxious to reach the goals set for them by parents and teachers.
- Children want to be more independent. They reach for new experiences and try to relate to a larger world.

Cognitive Characteristics

At Six

- They have a speaking vocabulary of over 2,500 words.
- Their attention span is likely to be short.
- They know number combinations up to 10 and the comparative values of common coins.
- They can define objects in terms of what they are used for.
- They know the right and left sides of the body.
- Their drawings are crude, but realistic.
- They will contribute to guided group planning.
- Their conversations usually are concerned with their own experiences and interests.
- These children's curiosity is active, and their memory is strong.
- They identify with imaginary characters.

At Seven

- Their attention span is still short, but they do not object to repetition. They can listen longer at seven than at six.
- Their reaction time is still slow.
- They are becoming more realistic and less imaginative.
- They can read some books themselves.
- They can reason, but they have little experience on which to base their judgments.
- They are just beginning to think abstractly.
- They are learning to evaluate the achievements of themselves and others.
- They are concerned with their own lack of skill and achievement.

chapter 4

The Games Approach to Teaching Basketball

Do you remember how as a child you were taught by adults to play a sport, either in an organized sports program or a physical education class? They probably taught you the basic skills using a series of drills that you found very boring. As you began to learn the basic skills, they eventually taught you the tactics of the game, showing you when to use these skills in various game situations. Do you remember how impatient you became during what seemed to be endless instruction, and how much you just wanted to play? Well, forget this traditional approach to teaching sports.

Can you recall learning a sport by playing with a group of your friends in the neighborhood? You didn't learn the basic skills first; there was no time for that. You began playing immediately. If you didn't know the basic things to do, your friends told you quickly during the game so they could keep playing. We're going to ask you to use a very similar approach, called the games approach, when you teach YMCA Rookies basketball. This approach knocks the socks off the traditional approach.

On the surface, teaching basketball by first teaching the basic skills of the sport and then the tactics of the game would seem to make sense, but we've discovered that this approach has two serious shortcomings. First, it teaches the skills of the sport out of the context of the game. Kids learn to pass and dribble the ball, but they find it difficult to learn how to use these skills within the game because they don't understand the tactics of the game. Second, learning skills by doing drills outside of the context of the game is so-o-o-o boring. The single biggest turnoff about adults teaching kids sports is that we over-organize the instruction and deprive kids of their intrinsic desire to play the game.

We're asking that you, as a YMCA Rookies coach, teach basketball the YMCA way, the games approach way. Clear the traditional approach out of your mind. Once you fully understand the games approach, you'll quickly see its superiority in teaching basketball. Not only will kids learn the game better, but you and they will also have much more fun. As a bonus, you'll have far fewer discipline problems.

With the games approach, all teaching of basketball skills begins by playing the game, usually a modified version of the game for younger children. As the children play the game, you help them learn what to do, what we call *tactical awareness*. When your players understand what they must do in the game, they are then eager to develop the skills to play the game. Now that players are motivated to learn the skills, you can demonstrate the skills of the game, have players practice using game-like drills, and provide individual instruction by identifying players' errors and helping to correct them.

In the traditional approach to teaching sports, players do this:

Learn the skill → Learn the tactics → Play the game

In the games approach players do this:

Play the game → Learn the tactics → Learn the skill

In the past we have placed too much emphasis on learning the skills and not enough on learning how to play skillfully—that is, how to use those skills during play. The games approach, in contrast, emphasizes learning what to do first, then how to do it. Moreover—and this is important—the games approach lets children discover what to do in the game, not by you telling them, but by them experiencing it. What you do as an effective coach is help them discover what they've experienced. In contrast to the "skill-drill-kill the enthusiasm" approach, the games approach is a guided discovery method of teaching. It empowers your children to solve the problems that arise in the game, and that's a big part of the fun in learning a game.

Now let's look more closely at the games approach to see the four-step process for teaching basketball:

1. Play a modified basketball game.
2. Help the players discover what they need to do to play the game successfully.
3. Teach the skills of the game.
4. Practice the skills in another game.

Step 1. Play a Modified Basketball Game

It's the first day of practice. Some of the kids are eager to get started; others are obviously apprehensive. Some have rarely dribbled a ball, most don't know the rules, and none know the positions in basketball. What do you do?

If you teach using the traditional approach, you start with a little warm-up activity, and then line them up for a simple dribbling drill and go from there. With the games approach, you begin by playing a modified game that is developmentally appropriate for the level of the players and also designed to focus on learning a specific part of the game.

Don't worry about modifying the game to be developmentally appropriate—we've done it for you. Our practice plans in part II are based on two- and three-player teams. We've also modified the size of the court, the height and size of the basket, the ball, and the rules. We'll tell you more about these changes later.

Modifying the game to place emphasis on a limited number of situations in the game is one way you guide your players to discover certain tactics in the game. For instance, you have your players play a two-versus-one basketball game, making the objective of the game learning to play with a teammate. Players can dribble only three times before passing the ball. Playing the game this way forces players to think about what they have to do to pass and receive accurately.

 ## Step 2. Help Players Discover What They Need to Do

As your players are playing the game, look for the right spot to "freeze" the action, step in, and hold a brief question-and-answer session to discuss problems they were having in carrying out the goal of the game. You don't need to pop in on the first miscue, but if they repeat the same types of mental or physical mistakes a few times in a row, step in and ask them questions that relate to the goal of the game and the necessary skills required. The best time to interrupt the game is when you notice that they are having trouble carrying out the main goal, or aim, of the game. By stopping the game, freezing action, and asking questions, you'll help them understand

- what the aim of the game is;
- what they must do to achieve that aim; and
- what skills they must use to achieve that aim.

After you've discussed the aim, you can begin the skill practice.

Here's an example of how to use questions in the games approach, continuing the example of the modified game we used earlier. Your players just played a game in which the objective was to play with a teammate. You see that they are having trouble doing this, so you interrupt the action and ask the following questions:

Coach: What would you do with the ball if you had a teammate?
Players: Pass to him or her.

Coach: What do you have to do to be successful at passing?
Players: Catch the ball and pass the ball right to my partner or teammate.

Coach: Why don't we try practicing passing and receiving?

Through the modified game and skillful questioning on your part, your players realize that accurate passing and receiving are essential to their success. Just as important, rather than telling them that these skills are critical, you led them to that discovery through a well-designed modified game and through questions. This questioning, which leads to players' discovery, is a crucial part of the games approach. Essentially you'll be asking your players—usually literally—"What do you need to do to succeed in this situation?"

Asking the right questions is a very important part of your teaching. We've given you sample questions in each practice plan (see chapters 6 and 7) to help you know where to begin. At first, asking questions will be difficult because your players have so little experience with the game. If you've learned sports through the traditional approach, you'll be tempted to tell your players how to play the game and not waste time asking them questions. Resist this powerful temptation to tell them what to do, and especially, don't tell them before they begin to play the game.

If your players have trouble understanding what to do, phrase your questions to let them choose between one option versus another. For example, if you ask them "What's the fastest way to get the ball down the court?" and get answers such as "Run with it" or "Toss it," then ask "Is it passing or dribbling?"

Sometimes players need to have more time playing the game, or you may need to make a further modification to the game so that it is easier for them to discover what they are to do. Using this discovery method takes more patience on your part, but it's a powerful way to learn. Don't be reluctant to change the numbers in the teams or some aspect of the structure of the game to aid this discovery. In fact, we advocate playing "lopsided" games (such as 3 v 1 or 3 v 2) in the second game of each practice; we'll explain this concept in a moment.

Step 3. Teach the Skills of the Game

Only when your players recognize the skills they need to execute the tactics they have come to learn from playing the game, do you want to teach the specific skills through focused drills. Now you can use a more traditional approach to teaching sports skills, called IDEA:

I Introduce the skill.

D Demonstrate the skill.

E Explain the skill.

A Attend to players practicing the skill.

Let's take a look at each part of the approach.

Introduce the Skill

Your players will already have some idea of what the skill is you want to teach because they've already tried it during a game and talked about it. Use this opportunity to get them focused on the specific skill. You can do this in three ways:

◎ **First, get their attention.** Make sure your players are positioned where they all should be able to see and hear you, and ask them if they can before you begin. Be sure that they are not facing the sun, a bright light, or some other distraction. When you speak, be enthusiastic, talk slightly louder than normal, and look your players in the eye.

◎ **Next, name the skill.** If the skill is referred to by more than one name, choose one and stick with it. Using consistent names for skills helps prevent confusion and makes it easier for you and your players to communicate.

◎ **Finally, briefly review how the skill will help them in the game.** They should have some idea from your earlier questioning, but make sure they see how it fits in the game and describe how the skill relates to more advanced skills.

Demonstrate the Skill

Players, especially younger ones, can learn a lot more from seeing the skill performed rather than just hearing about it. The skill must be shown correctly, so if you don't feel you can demonstrate it well, have another adult or a skilled player do it. Keep these tips in mind when demonstrating a skill:

◎ Use correct form.

◎ Demonstrate the skill several times.

◎ During one or two performances, slow down the action so players can see every movement involved in the skill.

◎ Perform the skill at different angles so your players can get a full perspective on it.

◎ Demonstrate the skill with both the right and the left hands.

Explain the Skill

Help your players understand what they see in the demonstration by giving them a short and simple explanation. Relate the skill to previously learned ones, when possible. To see whether your explanation is working, ask your players whether they understand it. A good way to do this is to have them repeat the explanation back to you. Ask questions such as "What are you going to do first?" "Then what?" and watch for players who look confused or uncertain. Try to explain the skill using different words, which may give players a different perspective.

Because you are working with young children, who have short attention spans, take no more than 3 minutes to do the introduction, demonstration, and explanation. Follow it immediately with practice.

Attend to Players Practicing the Skill

The practice plans in chapters 6 and 7 will provide you with specific ideas on how to run the practice, as well as cue words you should use during practice. Use these cues to help the players remember what to focus on during practice.

As your players practice, watch them closely to see which ones can use additional help. Some players will need you to physically guide them through the skill; this guidance will help them gain the confidence they need to try. Most will just need some feedback from you, and they'll be glad to get it—if you do it the right way.

Nobody likes to be yelled at, especially when they're supposed to be having fun! The young children you are working with have little or no prior experience with basketball or even sports in general. They also have not fully developed their motor skills, so you should expect to see more incorrect than correct movements during practice. If you lose your cool when a player makes a mistake, you're just teaching that player to stop trying or to get upset about errors—not exactly what you had in mind. Let your players know that making mistakes isn't the end of the world.

If you have to correct a player, be sure not to follow a positive statement with the word *but*. For example, don't say "Alesha, your dribbling is great, but you need to pass the ball more often." Saying it this way causes many kids to ignore the positive statement and focus on the negative one. Instead of the word *but*, use the word *and*. Say something such as "Alesha, your dribbling is great, and now let's work on passing."

Remember that praise from you is very motivational for your players. Be sure to tell them what they are doing right and help them correct what they are doing wrong.

Step 4. Practice the Skills in Another Game

Once the players have practiced the skill, you then put them in another game situation—this time a lopsided game (such as 3 v 1 or 3 v 2). Why use lopsided teams? It's simple: As a coach, you want your players to experience success as they're learning skills. The best way to experience success early on is to create an advantage for the players. This makes it more likely that, for instance, in a 3 v 1 game, your three offensive players will be able to make four passes before attempting to score.

When you get to the practice plans in chapters 6 and 7, you'll see that we often use even-sided games (3 v 3) in the first games and lopsided games in the second games. The reasoning behind this is to first introduce players to a situation similar to what they will experience in competition and let them discover the challenges they face in performing the necessary skill. Then you teach them the skill, have them practice it, and put them back in another game—this time a lopsided one to give them a greater chance of experiencing success.

As players improve their skills, you don't need to use lopsided games. At a certain point, having a 3 v 1 advantage will be too easy for the kids and won't challenge them to hone their skills. At that point you lessen the advantage to 3 v 2, or you may even decide that they're ready to practice the skill in even-sided competition. The key is to set up situations where your players experience success, yet are challenged in doing so. This will take careful monitoring on your part, but having kids play lopsided games as they are learning skills is a very effective way of helping them learn and improve.

So, that's the games approach. Your players will get to *play* more in practice, and once they learn how skills fits in with their performance and enjoyment of the game, they'll be more motivated to work on those skills, which will help them to be successful.

Part II
The Coaching Plans

Now you understand what your job is as a coach and the games approach to teaching basketball that we want you to use. In this part, we'll map out for you what we want you to teach players. In chapter 5, we'll present the season plans for what you'll teach the entire season, not just the skills and tactics, but also the rules and traditions, the fitness concepts, and a few key character development concepts. Then in chapter 6, we provide you with 10 practice plans for four- and five-year-olds, and in chapter 7, we provide 10 practice plans for six- to seven-year-olds. When you want to know more about how to teach a skill, a rule, a fitness concept, or a character concept listed in the practice plans, you'll find the information you need in part III.

chapter 5

The Season Plans

If you're feeling a bit overwhelmed by the job you've taken on, don't worry. In this chapter, we give you specific guidance on what to teach. This chapter will give you an overview of the curriculum for each of the two age groups; chapters 6 and 7 provide practice plans for each group.

The season plans we've laid out have five components:

- Purpose
- Tactics and skills
- Rules and traditions
- Fitness concepts
- Character development concepts

Here's a brief description of each component:

- **Purpose.** The purpose of the practice is your main focus.

- **Tactics and skills.** Tactics are knowing what to do during the game (and when to do it), and they require an understanding of the problems faced by each team during the game and how those problems can be solved. Ways to maintain possession of the ball would be tactics. Skills are the physical skills traditionally taught, such as passing or shooting the ball or controlling the ball during play.

- **Rules and traditions.** You will teach the rules of the sport to young children gradually, as part of playing games and learning skills. Traditions are those unwritten rules that players follow to be courteous and safe, such as raising your hand when you foul someone or playing cooperatively with the others on your team.

- **Fitness concepts.** Even young children can understand some simple concepts about health and fitness, such as the idea that exercise strengthens your heart, so some of these are suggested as the focus for brief discussions during practice.

◎ **Character development concepts.** The four core values—caring, honesty, respect, and responsibility—can all be related to many situations that arise while playing basketball. For example, playing cooperatively with teammates shows that you care about them. Again, we'll suggest some specific ideas for briefly discussing character development values.

Basketball Curriculum for Four- and Five-Year-Olds

At this age, children need understanding and skills to enable them to play a game. From a tactical perspective, you need to help them to see the need to keep the ball, to shoot baskets, and to try to stop their opponents from scoring. The outline on page 31 provides a weekly guide and addresses tactical and skill components, and other activities that will be detailed in the practice plans.

Basketball Curriculum for Six- and Seven-Year-Olds

Using a small number of players on a team with the three-versus-three game allows players to continue to have many tactical options without the pressure of large numbers of opponents. This arrangement makes it more likely that players will attempt to pass, dribble, or shoot as the need arises. Progressing from the four- and five-year-old age group, players can now revisit the tactical components of possession and attack while adding a closer look at defending. The outline on page 32 provides a weekly guide that shows the tactical and skill components, as well as the rules and character development components. These components will all be detailed in the practice plans. Boys and girls should still play together at this age level.

YMCA Rookies Basketball Season Plan

Four- to Five-Year-Olds

Week	Purpose	Tactics and skills	Rules and traditions	Fitness concepts	Character development concepts
1	Playing the 1 v 1 game—boundaries, rules	Starting and restarting the game Dribbling Play cooperative defense	Start and restart rules Modified rules Keep control rule	**General fitness** Participation in sport is good.	**Four core values** The four core values are introduced.
2	Playing the 1 v 1 game under control Handling the ball	Dribbling under control		**Cardiorespiratory fitness** Your heart is a muscle.	**Responsibility to others** Players should stay under control.
3	Keeping possession of the ball	Passing and receiving	Unwritten rule Being a good sport	**Muscular strength and endurance** Playing basketball strengthens leg muscles.	**Honesty** If you break a rule, raise your hand and tell the coach.
4	Keeping possession of the ball	Dribbling and passing to a partner (chest pass, bounce pass)		**Safety and rules** Follow the rules.	**Caring** Take turns with teammates.
5	Attacking the basket	Shooting with basic technique Shooting close to the basket	Modified double dribble rule Scoring points—1 point for hitting the rim/backboard; 2 points for getting the ball in the basket	**Healthy habits** Eat nutritious foods and get enough sleep.	**Caring** Support teammates when they make a mistake.
6	Keeping possession of the ball and attacking the basket Dribbling and driving to shoot	Starting, stopping, and changing direction quickly while dribbling Jump stop	Modified traveling rule	**Flexibility** Stretching muscles makes them flexible.	**Responsibility** It's important that everyone work hard during practice.
7	Keeping possession of the ball	Ballhandling Dribbling under control		**Muscular strength and endurance** Your arm muscles get stronger when you practice dribbling.	**Respect** Respect your opponents.
8	Keeping possession of the ball	Dribbling under pressure		**Training and conditioning** Being active outside of practice is important.	**Responsibility** Listen to the coach and share team duties.
9	Defending your own space	Basic defensive technique	Modified foul rule	**Muscular strength and endurance** Playing basketball strengthens thigh muscles.	**Respect for opponent** Shake hands with opponents at the end of a game.
10	Playing a 3 v 3 game Keeping possession of the ball	Passing and receiving Supporting teammate with the ball		**Healthy habits** List and discuss the habits that should be part of daily routine.	**Keeping perspective on the game** Learn and have fun while playing.

YMCA Rookies Basketball Season Plan

Six- to Seven-Year-Olds

Week	Purpose	Tactics and skills	Rules and traditions	Fitness concepts	Character development concepts
1	Keeping possession of the ball	Ball handing and dribbling under control Play cooperative defense	Start and restart rules Modified rules	**General fitness** Being active leads to fitness.	**Four core values** The four core values are introduced.
2	Keeping possession of the ball	Dribbling under pressure Dribbling and passing to a partner	Unwritten rule: Being a good sport Modified traveling rule	**Flexibility** Stretching muscles makes them flexible.	**Responsibility** Learn the team motto: Play hard, play fair, and have fun!
3	Attacking the basket	Shooting with basic technique Shooting close to basket	Modified double dribble rule	**Cardiorespiratory fitness** The heart is a special muscle that pumps blood.	**Respect for others** It's important to be a good sport.
4	Keeping possession of the ball Attacking the basket Dribbling and driving to shoot	Starting, stopping and changing direction quickly while dribbling Jump stop		**Cardiorespiratory fitness** Our heartbeat increases with exercise.	**Honesty** Raise your hand when you commit a foul.
5	Keeping possession of the ball	Dribbling under pressure		**Cardiorespiratory fitness** Your heart gets stronger when you exercise and play.	**Responsibility** Mistakes are okay. Don't make excuses for your play.
6	Playing a 3 v 2 game Keeping possession of the ball	Pass, receive, and support under pressure Play active defense	Possession rule	**Flexibility** Stretching muscles makes them flexible.	**Caring** Take turns with teammates.
7	Defending your own space	Defending an opponent	Modified foul rule	**Muscle strength and endurance** Physical activity gives you strong legs and arms.	**Responsibility** Keep control of yourself during practice and games.
8	Defending your own space Pressing the ball handler	Pressuring the ball handler Stealing the ball	Principle of verticality Regular half-court rules	**General fitness** We need to keep active every day, even days we have no practice.	**Responsibility to team** It's important to value teamwork.
9	Attacking the basket	Shooting within 5–8 feet of basket Receiving a pass and shooting accurately		**General fitness** Healthy eating habits give you more energy.	**Caring** Forgive mistakes; they are part of the game.
10	Playing a 3 v 3 game Maintaining possession of the ball	Passing quickly and accurately Supporting the ball handler	Field goal is two points	**General fitness** Eat good foods rather than junk foods.	**Respect for game** Realize it takes years to master some skills.

chapter 6

Practice Plans for Four- to Five-Year-Olds

This chapter contains 10 practice plans to use with your four- to five-year-old YMCA Rookies basketball players. Before we get to those, though, we'll explain how basketball is modified for YMCA Rookies and give you a quick review of what's in the practice plans and how they are to be used.

 ## Game Modifications

All games for four- to five-year-olds will be played on a half-court or short courts (see figure 6.1) with modified rules (see chapter 9 for basketball rules). Because young players have to learn about violations (such as forgetting to dribble the ball while moving) and fouls (illegal contact with an opposing player) gradually, the rules for YMCA Rookies basketball have the following modifications:

- Players are to follow a self-space rule, which has three parts:
  — Players may not block shots or touch the ball when the ballhandler is holding the ball, but they may steal the ball when it is passed or dribbled.
  — Defending players may not intentionally get in the path of an offensive player to take a defensive charge.

—Defending players may not undercut an offensive player who is shooting an uncontested layup. This rule minimizes fouls and controls playing defense.

- Only player-to-player defense is used, not zones.
- No shot clock or scoreboard is used.
- Players are to follow a keep control rule, which says that players must keep physical control of their bodies and the ball. No rough play is allowed.
- All players must be good sports and show respect. Players who show unsporting conduct should be penalized by being removed from the game for a time.

Games may be played in one of two ways:

1. **Modified half-court games.** Individual players (1 v 1) or teams (2 v 1, 2 v 2, 3 v 2, or 3 v 3) take turns trying to score, and then switch roles from offense to defense or vice versa.

2. **Short-court games.** Short-court games require baskets at the sides of a regular basketball court. Each short court is half of a regulation-size court, but players run across it widthwise, rather than lengthwise. Using a short court is best for developing skills in younger players.

For four- and five-year-olds, use modified half-court rules throughout the season. Even in the short-court game, teams should alternate being the offensive or defensive team, just as they do for modified half-court.

During game play, be sure to rotate partners (opponents). You can arrange several short games (three to five minutes) and rotate partners at the beginning of each new game. Remember that changing partners changes the game. Have no more than seven players to a team.

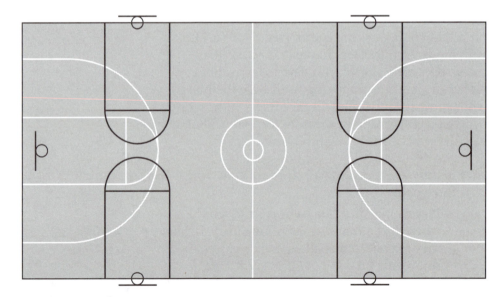

Figure 6.1   Crosscourt playing area.

Having the right amount and type of equipment is critical to the success of the YMCA Rookies program. All aspects of the game must be modified to fit this level. Table 6.1 gives you some examples.

To help players learn, you can work with players in two ways:

◎ Teach by invitation. Adjust for individual differences in players by inviting the players to decide some of the parameters of the practice situation themselves, such as choosing the size of the ball.

◎ Vary the parameters of the practice yourself in order to make play easier or more challenging for individuals or small groups.

Using either strategy allows players to succeed while being challenged; play isn't too hard or too easy.

To simplify the game or to increase the challenge for players, try the following:

◎ Change the size and weight of the ball.

◎ Change the size and height of the basket.

◎ Give players timed goals, and then increase or decrease the interval or duration.

◎ Give players trial goals, and then increase or decrease the number of times the skill must be done successfully.

In the YMCA Rookies basketball program, players focus on skills related to offense. Defensive skills are important, but if those skills are introduced too soon, players may have difficulty developing offensive skills, especially if their peers play defense aggressively. Introduce defensive skills after players have

TABLE 6.1

Modified Factors in Basketball

Factors	YMCA Rookies basketball
Size and weight of ball	Junior #5
Height of basket	5 feet—bushel baskets or wash baskets hung on the walls work well
Size of basket	Large to regulation
Number of players	Small sided (1 v 1, 2 v 1, 2 v 2, 3 v 2, 3 v 3)
Court size	Half-court, short court
Number of players per team	7

developed some proficiency with off- and on-the-ball skills. Rather than eliminating defense, we recommend that you control defensive play by using two levels of involvement:

1. Cooperative defense (cold). The player assumes a defensive posture two arm lengths from the opponent and is relatively passive.

2. Active defense (warm). The player assumes a defensive posture about one and a half arm lengths from the opponent, has active hands and feet, but makes no attempts to intercept the ball.

Players who are four to five years old should use cooperative defense; players who are six to seven years old start out using cooperative defense and then move to active defense.

Here are some other ways to make practice games simpler or more challenging:

- Equally increase or decrease the number of players suggested (for example, if we suggest playing 2 v 2, make it simpler by playing 1 v 1, or make it more challenging by playing 3 v 3).
- Begin with *no* defense.
- Add an extra offensive player to make it easier for the offense (for example, 3 v 2 instead of 2 v 2).
- Add an extra defender to make it harder on the offense (for example, 2 v 3 instead of 3 v 3) once players have acquired the skills they need to be successful.
- Perform the skill or game at a slower than normal pace to make it simpler.
- Increase or decrease the number of passes you require before the offense can attempt a shot.

All these suggested modifications will help your YMCA Rookies players develop their basketball skills at a level at which they can succeed. As they become more skilled, the game rules will become more like those of the official game. YMCA Rookies practices will give your players a good foundation to build on as they grow.

 Practice Plan Organization

Each plan contains the following sections:

- Purpose
- Equipment
- Practice Plan
- Coach's Point
- Variations

Purpose focuses on what you want to teach your players during that practice; it is your main theme for the day. *Equipment* notes what you'll need on hand for that practice. We'll address the *Practice Plan* in depth in just a moment. The *Coach's Point* lists helpful reminders for you, points of emphasis to most effectively conduct the practice. We include *Variations* to games at the end of each plan, providing you with modifications to keep skill practices and games fun and interesting and to help players of varying skill levels.

The Practice Plan section outlines what you will do during each practice session. It consists of these elements:

- Warm-Up
- Fitness Circle
- Game 1
- Skill Practices and Games
- Team Circle and Wrap-up

You'll begin each session with 5 to 10 minutes of warm-up activities. (Note: All times given in the practice plans are approximate.) This warm-up will be followed by five minutes of the Fitness Circle, during which you briefly talk with players about an idea that relates to health or fitness. Then, in Game 1, you'll be working on the first two steps of the four-step process for teaching basketball: having players play a modified basketball game and helping them discover what they need to do. The game will be designed to focus players' attention on a particular aspect of basketball. Start the game but, when it's clear that the players are having trouble achieving the goal of the game, stop the game and ask questions and get answers similar to those shown in the plans. The questions and answers will help the players see what skills they need to solve tactical problems in the game.

The third part of the four-step process of teaching basketball is teaching the skills identified in Game 1 through the skill practices. In each skill practice, you'll use the IDEA approach, which means you do the following actions:

I Introduce the skill.

D Demonstrate the skill.

E Explain the skill.

A Attend to players practicing the skill.

Chapter 8 contains descriptions of all the skills, so we give you a page reference in the skill practices to guide you to the appropriate description. The introduction, demonstration, and explanation should be very brief to fit young children's short attention spans. As the players practice, you will attend to individual children and guide them with teaching cues or further demonstration.

After the skill practices, you will have the children play another game to finish the four-step process. This lets them use the skills they just learned and helps them understand how to utilize those skills in the context of a game. Note that in Game 1, when players are being introduced to a new tactic or skill, they usually will play an even-sided game (such as 3 v 3). This allows them to encounter the challenges they will face in executing the tactic or skill. Then, in most Game 2s, they play lopsided games (such as 3 v 1 or 3 v 2) to increase their chances of experiencing success and beginning to master the new tactic or skill. However, if your players are showing proficiency with the new tactic or skill, you can use even-sided games in Game 2. The choice is yours; for more on this issue, see chapter 4.

Each practice plan concludes with a Team Circle, which focuses on character development. You will take about five minutes to talk to your players about some aspect of basketball that relates to one of the four core values: caring, honesty, respect, and responsibility. Following this talk, you'll wrap up the practice with a reminder of the next practice day and time and a preview of what will be taught in the next practice session.

Note that Fitness and Team Circles are meant to be true discussions, not lectures where you do all the talking and the players do all the listening. Ask the questions provided and wait for your players to respond. Don't feed them the answers that we provide; these answers are meant to help you guide the discussion only. Your role is as much to ask questions and get players to respond as it is to dole out information.

The plans in this chapter, combined with the information in the rest of this book, should give you what you need to lead practices. Just remember to be patient and caring as you work on skills. Different children will progress at different rates, and it's more important that they learn the sport in a positive way than it is that they learn quickly.

Practice 1

Warm-Up (10 minutes)

Begin each practice with 5 to 10 minutes of warm-up activities to get players loosened up and ready to go.

1. Players free dribble and handle the ball in space (one ball per player), using an area no larger than half-court.
2. Players dribble and shoot at a target: a hoop mounted against the wall, a bushel basket at a low height against the wall, or a square or circle taped on the wall.

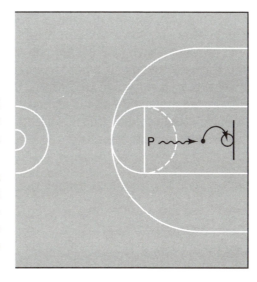

👉 PURPOSE

To play a 1 v 1 game, focusing on boundaries and rules and dribbling. The objective is for players to be able to play a 1 v 1 game of basketball in a predetermined area while following simple start and restart rules.

Equipment

- ☑ One basketball per player
- ☑ One portable basket per two players (if possible)
- ☑ Tape (optional)

Fitness Circle (5 minutes)

Following the warm-up, gather the players and briefly discuss the fitness concept for that practice.

Key Idea: General fitness

Gather children into a group. "Everyone jump 10 times. Our muscles help us jump. When you use your muscles a long time without getting too tired, it improves your *endurance*, which means you can run longer without getting tired. Now run really fast to the free throw line and back." Wait for them to return. "Running strengthens your heart and lungs. Now touch your toes; try to keep your fingers down there while I count to 10. Stretching makes you flexible, like a rubber band. When we play basketball, our bodies run, jump, and move. It makes our bodies stronger and improves our fitness, which means we can run and play longer and faster. Having good physical fitness is important for basketball and for being healthy. Every practice we'll talk about fitness in our Fitness Circles.

"At the beginning of each practice, after the warm-up, we'll have a Fitness Circle. The Fitness Circle is a time during which we will learn more about how basketball makes you healthy and fit and how being healthy and fit helps you play better basketball."

Practice 1 (cont'd)

COACH's point

☞ Spend time getting players to understand how to play a modified half-court game. These games are more cooperative than competitive, limiting players' focus to boundaries, starting and restarting game play, and keeping control. Be flexible regarding violations (such as double dribbling or traveling); however, you will need a keep control rule. For example, if a player just picks up the ball and starts running with it without dribbling, that would be out of control. Teach cooperative (cold) defense to the players.

Game 1 (10 minutes)

Following the Fitness Circle, get the kids playing a game. After letting the players play for awhile, interrupt the game for a time of questions and answers—with YOU asking the questions and your PLAYERS providing the answers (about what the goal of the game was and what skills and tactics they needed to perform to succeed in the game). For many games, we provide diagrams or figures showing how the game is played. We also often provide "coach's points" for you to pass along to your players during the games.

Goal

Players will learn that they have to attack the basket (target) to score in basketball.

Description

1 v 1, modified half-court—Explain how to start and restart the game. Each player attempts to dribble and shoot at a target. His or her opponent plays cooperative defense. No traveling or double dribble violations are called.

You'll follow Game 1 with a Skill Practice, during which you'll introduce, demonstrate, and explain a skill or tactic, and then attend to your players as they practice it. The question-and-answer session, in which your players tell YOU what skills and tactics they needed to be successful in the game, leads directly to the Skill Practice. We often provide coaching points with the Skill Practices; pass these points along to your players. We also provide "coaching cues"—phrases to help your players focus on the task at hand—during many Skill Practices and Games.

Coach: What are you trying to do?
Players: Score a basket (or put the ball into the target).

Coach: What do you have to do to get the ball close to the basket (target)?
Players: Dribble and run.

Skill Practice 1 (10 minutes)

1. Introduce, demonstrate, and explain how to dribble without losing control (see pages 121–122).
2. Have your players practice dribbling without losing control.

Description

Individual—Players should stand apart from each other (allow 15 seconds for them to move to their own space); on a signal, they begin dribbling around the court without losing control. Players stop and catch the ball quickly on a signal. Repeat three times using short intervals (20, 30, and 45 seconds).

Practice 1

COACH's cues

"Use your fingerpads."
"Keep your eyes over the ball."
"Keep the ball low."
"Keep the ball at your side."

Skill Practice 2 (15 minutes)

Description

Individual—Each player practices dribbling. Players can choose the size and weight of the ball they use.

Easier Activities

- Dribbling with one hand.
- Dribbling continuously with left and right hands.
- Striking a ball down and catching it.

More Difficult Activities

- Dribbling and moving with the ball.
- Dribbling in different places around the body while stationary.
- Dribbling continuously while switching hands.
- Dribbling at different heights.

Game 2 (5 minutes)

Goal

Players will use boundaries and rules and will dribble in game play.

Description

Same as Game 1.

Practice 1 (cont'd)

Team Circle (5 minutes)

Conclude practice by gathering your players and discussing a character development concept. These aren't lectures; you want your players' active participation in these discussions. Following the discussions, wrap up the practice with a few comments.

Key Idea: Four core values

Gather children into a circle. "This season we'll talk about four qualities of a good person and teammate. Number one is *caring*. Can you tell me ways you show caring to others? Helping someone up when they fall? Good! Number two is *honesty*. What ways do you show honesty? How about if you tell someone if you played with their game or toy? That's honesty. Number three is *respect*. Do you know what respect is? One thing that shows respect is listening to adults when they speak to you, like you're doing now. Number four is *responsibility*. One way to show you're responsible is to pick up after yourself. Don't wait for others to pick up for you." Ask them to share ways they show the four values in other areas of their lives. "Good teammates show these values to each other. We'll talk more about these four values during the season."

Wrap-Up

Make summary comments about practice. Remind players of the next practice day and time and give them a sneak preview of that practice—handling the ball and dribbling.

Variations

In working with the players on levels of dribbling proficiency, you can vary the activity depending on the developmental needs of the player.

To Simplify
- Skill Practice 1: Keep the interval short (10, 12, or 15 seconds).
- Skill Practice 2: Let players use a ball of a size and weight that allows them to succeed.
- Games 1 and 2: Use a large-size basket or target and/or place the basket or target low.

To Challenge
- Skill Practice 1: Lengthen the interval.
- Skill Practice 2: Let players use a ball of a size and weight that will challenge them.
- Games 1 and 2: Increase the height of the basket or target.

Practice 2

Warm-Up (10 minutes)

Individual—Players should stand apart from each other (allow 15 seconds for them to move to their own space); on a signal, they begin dribbling around the court without losing control. Players stop and catch the ball quickly on a signal. Repeat this exercise three times in short intervals (20, 30, and 45 seconds).

Fitness Circle (5 minutes)

Key Idea: Cardiorespiratory fitness

Gather children into a group. "Everyone hold one hand up and make a fist. Squeeze your fist tightly, then let go. Keep tightening and letting go." Children continue for 10 counts. "Your heart is a special muscle that tightens and relaxes just like your fist is doing. Your heart is about the size of your fist. Let's put our fists over our chests. Every time it tightens, or beats, your heart pumps blood all over your body. When you run during basketball, your heart beats faster. The beat slows down when you slow down. Let's run with high knees for 15 counts while we count together. Stop and feel your heartbeat by putting your hand over your chest." Model for players. "Running strengthens your heart and lungs and improves your fitness."

Game 1 (10 minutes)

Goal

Players will attack the basket (target) to score in basketball.

Description

1 v 1, modified half-court game—Each player attempts to dribble and shoot at a basket (or target). His or her opponent plays cooperative defense. Players earn a point if they attempt a shot close to the basket (or target). Designate the area (such as the lane) from which players must shoot to earn a point. Do not call any traveling or double dribble violations.

👉 PURPOSE

To play a 1 v 1 game, focusing on playing the game under control. The objective is for players to be able to handle the ball and dribble under control.

Equipment

- ✓ One basketball per player (if possible)
- ✓ One portable basket per two players
- ✓ Tape or cones as markers (optional)

👉 Modifying is the key to success with this age group. Keep asking yourself, "How can I modify this and still have the basic principles of basketball?"

Practice 2 (cont'd)

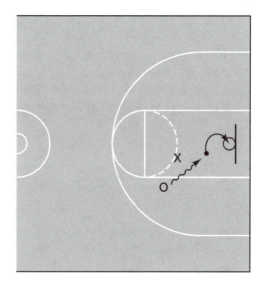

Coach: What is the goal of the game?
Players: The goal is to score a basket (put the ball into the target).

Coach: How do you move toward the basket (or target) with the ball?
Players: We move by dribbling and running, by dribbling under control.

Skill Practice (20 minutes)

Description

Individual—Each player practices dribbling. Players can choose the size and weight of the ball they use. Have them try the following activities:

- Dribbling and moving with the ball.
- Dribbling in different places around the body while stationary.
- Dribbling continuously while switching hands.
- Dribbling at different heights.

COACH's cues

"Use your fingerpads."
"Keep your eyes over the ball."
"Keep the ball low."
"Keep the ball at your side."

44

Practice 2

Game 2 (10 minutes)

Goal

Players will keep possession of the ball using a dribble in a game.

Description

Same as Game 1, except that players earn one point for a shot attempt and one point for dribbling under control. (Players determine whether they achieved one or two points; if the ball did not slip out of their hands as they played, it was dribbled under control.)

Team Circle (5 minutes)

Key Idea: Responsibility

Gather children into a group. "I want us all to pretend we're eggs. Eggs have shells that can break. What would happen if we bumped into each other as eggs? Right. We would crack and break. Let's move around the court being eggs. Don't bump each other or we'll break!" Continue this exercise for about one minute. "We were all careful not to bump each other so our 'shells' wouldn't break! That was great! You were in charge of or 'responsible' for your moving. When we're careful of each other, we're responsible for our space and other players' space. This shows responsibility during practice and games."

Wrap-Up

Make summary comments about practice. Remind players of the next practice day and time and give them a sneak preview of that practice—passing and receiving the basketball.

Variations

When working with the players on levels of dribbling proficiency, you can vary the activity depending on the developmental needs of the player. You can establish an accountability check, in which you or a player's peer witnesses a demonstration of proficiency for each activity.

45

Practice 3

☞ PURPOSE

To keep possession of the ball, focusing on passing and receiving. The objective is for players to be able to pass and receive the basketball.

Equipment

 One basketball per player

 One portable basket per two players (if possible)

 Tape or cones as markers (optional)

Warm-Up (10 minutes)

Individual—Each player has a ball to practice dribbling. Have them try the following activities:

- Dribbling and moving with the ball.
- Dribbling in different places around the body while stationary.
- Dribbling continuously while switching hands.
- Dribbling at different heights.

Fitness Circle (5 minutes)

Key Idea: Muscular strength and endurance

Gather children into a circle. "Everyone find your own space so that you don't bump your neighbor. You're going to run in your own spot for 30 seconds, then stop. Ready, go!" Time children and verbally let them know the time remaining; stop them at the end of the time. "What part of the body did we just use the most when we ran?" Encourage their responses. "When we play basketball, which part of the body do we use the most?" Wait for their responses. "Muscles in our body help us to move our legs. Playing basketball will help our leg muscles get stronger and grow bigger."

Practice 3

Game 1 (10 minutes)

Goal

Pairs of players will play as a team.

Description

2 v 1, modified half-court game—Two players become partners and play against one defensive player, then one partner must switch roles with the defensive player. Switch at least twice so all players get to play defense. Limit them to dribbling three times before passing. Do not call any traveling or double dribble violations.

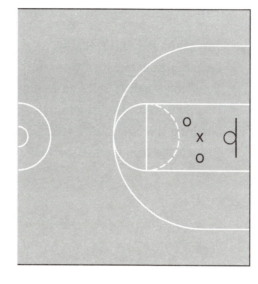

Explain to players that they are expected to be good sports and to show respect to other players. If a player shows unsporting conduct, he or she will be removed from the game for a few minutes.

Coach: What would you do with the ball if you had a teammate?
Players: Pass to him or her.

Coach: What do you have to do to be successful at passing?
Players: Catch the ball and pass the ball right to my partner or teammate.

Skill Practice (20 minutes)

1. Introduce, demonstrate, and explain how to pass and receive (see pages 119–121).
2. Have your players practice passing and receiving.

☞ You may have to spend more time on basic receiving and passing skills.

Practice 3 (cont'd)

Description

Individual or pairs—Demonstrate throwing and catching, and then have players practice some of the following throwing and catching activities:

- Tossing to self and catching.
- Catching from a skilled thrower.
- Bouncing a ball to self and catching it.
- Passing or throwing to a target.
- Catching the ball in different places around the body.
- Passing the ball against the wall and catching it.

COACH's cues

for receiving
"Target the hands."
"Keep your eyes on the ball."
"Reach for it."
"Pull it in."

for passing
"Put your hands on the sides of the ball, with your thumbs pointing to each other."
"Step forward with your preferred foot."
"Push the ball forward at chest level, elbows out, and snap it."

(After the pass) "Move your thumbs down, backs of your hands facing each other, and move your weight forward."

Game 2 (10 minutes)

Goal

Pairs of players will play as a team.

Description

Same as Game 1.

Practice 3

Team Circle (5 minutes)

Key Idea: Honesty

Gather children into a group near two cones about 10 feet apart. "Can you step out of bounds when you have the basketball? What if it's an accident and nobody saw you? Those of you who think it's okay to step out of bounds, stand by this cone. Those who think it's not okay, stand by this one." Wait for children to choose. Then ask them why they chose the cone they did. "Stepping out of bounds, even if it's an accident, is against the rules. What should you do if it happens? Those of you who think you should just keep playing, stay at this cone; those of you who think you should tell the coach and give the ball to the other team, go stand by that cone." Wait for everyone to finish choosing. "It's important to be honest. If you step out of bounds with the ball, even if nobody sees it, tell the coach and give the ball to the other team."

Wrap-Up

Make summary comments about practice. Remind players of the next practice day and time and give them a sneak preview of that practice—dribbling and passing the ball to a partner.

Variations

To simplify or to increase the challenge, modify the ball (size and weight) and basket (height and size) to meet players' needs.

☞ Remember to use teaching by invitation or to vary the game parameters yourself.

Practice 4

PURPOSE

To keep possession of the ball, focusing on dribbling and passing the ball to a partner. The objective is for the players to be able to execute both the chest and bounce pass.

Equipment

- ☑ One basketball per player
- ☑ One portable basket per two players (if possible)
- ☑ Tape or cones as markers (optional)

Warm-Up (10 minutes)

Individual—Players dribble in different pathways:

- Move in straight, curved, and zigzag pathways in general space.
- Follow the straight lines on the gym floor.
- Move in a straight pathway. Each time a player meets another player or hears your signal, he or she turns quickly to the right or left and continues dribbling.
- Move throughout general space, quickly moving from side to side in a zigzag.

Fitness Circle (5 minutes)

Key Idea: Safety and rules

Gather children into a circle. "What are the easiest ways to get hurt while playing basketball?" Wait for answers (slipping and falling, getting poked in the eye, getting hit in the face with a pass). "What's the best way to keep from getting hurt? How do we prevent these accidents from happening?" Point out that while no sport is injury free, their risks of being hurt are much reduced when they follow the rules and care about each other.

Practice 4

Game 1 (10 minutes)

Goal

Pairs of players will play as a team.

Description

2 v 1, modified half-court game—Two players become partners and play against one defensive player, then one player must switch roles with the defensive player. Switch at least twice so all players get to play defense. Limit players to dribbling three times before passing. Do not call any traveling or double dribble violations.

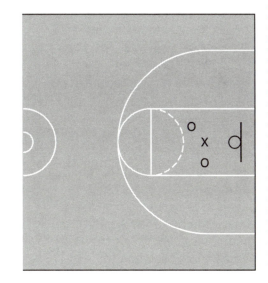

Coach: What is the goal of the game?
Players: The goal is to keep the ball to score or to dribble and pass to score.

Coach: What types of passes are there? (This question is to see how much players know about passing.)
Players: Two types of passes are the bounce pass and the chest pass.

Skill Practice 1 (10 minutes)

1. Introduce, demonstrate, and explain how to chest pass and bounce pass (see page 120).
2. Have your players practice chest passes and bounce passes.

Description

Pairs—Players practice passing to each other. After they have passed the ball four times, they change partners.

COACH's cues

for chest pass

"Keep your chest high."
"Keep your thumbs down and together."
"Step forward."

for bounce pass

"Snap your thumbs down and together."
"Bounce the ball so your partner catches it waist high."
"Step forward."

☞ Encourage players to move when they dribble.

☞ Remind passers to pass a little in front of their partners.

51

Practice 4 (cont'd)

Skill Practice 2 (10 minutes)

1. Introduce, demonstrate, and explain how to dribble and pass to a partner (see pages 119–122).
2. Have your players practice dribbling and passing to a partner.

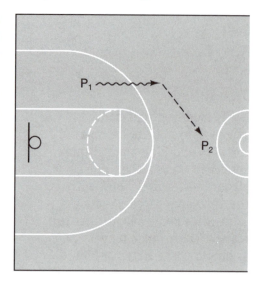

Description

Pairs—Partner 1 dribbles the ball 8 to 10 times and then passes it to partner 2. Partner 2 starts dribbling forward and then passes back to partner 1. The partners continue to dribble and pass to each other from one end of the gym to the other. The goal is to make four successful passes in a row (adjust number as necessary).

COACH's cues

"If you have the ball, you must dribble to move."
"Pass on the move."
"Control the ball."
"Lead your partner."

Game 2 (10 minutes)

Goal
Players will play in offensive teams of two, dribbling and passing in a game.

Description
Same as Game 1, except choose either 2 v 1 or 2 v 2. Rotate players accordingly so they all have a chance to play offense and defense.

Practice 4

Team Circle (5 minutes)

Key Idea: Caring

Gather children into a circle. Stand in the middle of the group with a ball. Pass to each child and give him or her a turn to pass back to you. "I am going to pass the ball. If a pass comes to you, pass the ball back to me." Work around the whole circle. Talk to the children about playing and learning when they come to practice. "Who had a turn to touch the ball?" Wait for their responses. "I made sure everyone had a chance to touch the ball. Raise your hand if it felt good to be able to have a turn. How would you have felt if you did not have a turn?" Listen to their responses. "We need to share the ball and take turns so everyone can learn and play. Sharing and taking turns show you care."

Wrap-Up

Make summary comments about practice. Remind players of the next practice day and time and give them a sneak preview of that practice—shooting the ball.

Variations

- To simplify skill practice, limit the number of practice activities or limit the practice to the chest pass only.
- To increase the challenge during games, have players pass only and not dribble.

Practice 5

👉 PURPOSE

To attack the basket, focusing on shooting close to the basket. The objective is for players to shoot using basic technique.

Equipment

- ☑ One basketball per player (if possible)
- ☑ One portable basket per two players (if possible)
- ☑ Tape or cones as markers

Warm-Up (10 minutes)

Pairs—Partners play follow-the-leader in single file while dribbling (have players leave three feet between them); they should switch who leads frequently.

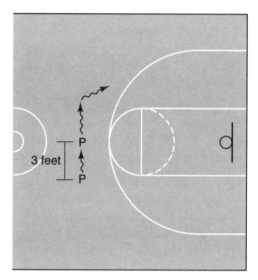

Fitness Circle (5 minutes)

Key Idea: Healthy habits

Gather children in a circle. "Do you know that when your body doesn't eat healthy foods and get enough sleep it moves slowly. Let's pretend we have no energy to move because we didn't eat enough healthy foods or get enough sleep." Begin to move slowly and encourage the children to follow. Move extremely slowly. "Everyone stop. Now I am going to fill your bodies up with healthy foods." Act out giving them foods. "Pretend we are sleeping. When I say 'Wake up!' you can move faster because you have enough energy and enough rest. Wake up and move faster. Stop! What are some other healthy habits you have learned?" Examples: daily exercise, brushing teeth, saying no to drugs, no smoking. "It's important for everyone to practice healthy habits."

Practice 5

Game 1 (10 minutes)

Goals

Players score by shooting in a 2 v 2 game.

Description

2 v 2, modified half-court game—Players earn one point if they hit the backboard or the rim of a modified basket and two points if it goes into the basket. Designate the area (such as the lane) from which players must shoot to earn points. Call modified double dribble violations. For example, a player can stop and start toward the basket three times before it is a violation. If a violation occurs, the player's opponent takes a turn.

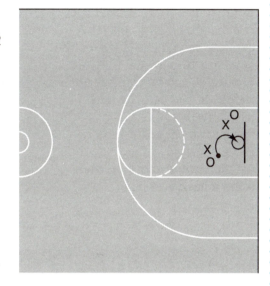

Coach: What is the goal of this game?
Players: The goal is to shoot at the basket and score points.

Coach: How do you do that?
Players: You shoot close to the basket.

Skill Practice (20 minutes)

1. Introduce, demonstrate, and explain how to shoot baskets with a set shot (see pages 122–125).
2. Have your players practice shooting baskets with a set shot.

Description

Individuals or pairs—Players can practice shooting individually or in pairs in a game of Around the Key. For this game, mark shooting spots with tape in an arc around the basket (inside the key). All shots should

☞ Limit the number of teaching cues you provide when you model and teach shooting.

Practice 5 (cont'd)

be close to the basket. Each player moves from spot to spot in order, shooting at each spot. If pairs are playing, player 2 gets the rebound and passes the ball back to player 1. The keys to success will be the size and weight of the ball the player uses as well as the height and size of the basket or target. Players should "high five" their partners when those partners score a basket.

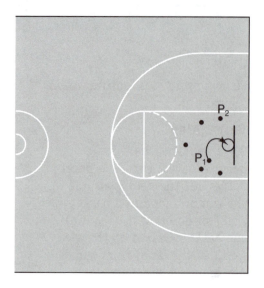

COACH's cues

"Keep hands apart on the ball."
"Only fingers touch the ball."
"Keep palms up."
"Point elbows toward the basket."
"Flip the wrist and wave good-bye." (The hand follows through after the shot.)

Game 2 (10 minutes)

Goal

Players score by shooting.

Description

Same as Game 1, except choose either 2 v 1 or 2 v 2, depending on the skill proficiency of your players. Rotate players accordingly so they all have a chance to play offense and defense. (See chapter 4 for more on the use of lopsided games.)

Practice 5

Team Circle (5 minutes)

Key Idea: Caring

Gather children into a group about 10 feet from a basket. "Let's pretend we're playing a basketball game. Watch what I do with the ball." Tell a child in the group you're passing to him. Make a bad pass. "That pass wasn't very good, was it? What would you say to me so that I don't feel bad about the pass?" As children respond, have each player who makes a supportive comment try to make a basket. If players make unsupportive comments, encourage them to change their words to become more supportive; after they have changed the words, have each of them try to make a basket. "It's very important to support your teammates, especially when they make mistakes. Saying something that makes someone feel good shows you care."

Wrap-Up

Make summary comments about practice. Remind players of the next practice day and time and give them a sneak preview of that practice—driving and dribbling to shoot.

COACH's point

☞ Find simple methods for helping players keep track of their progress; children at this age will vary in their ability to count and keep score. For example, you could award a token to a player each time he or she achieves a goal.

Practice 6

☞ PURPOSE

To keep possession of the ball and attack the basket, focusing on driving and dribbling to shoot. The objective is for players to be able to start and stop, change directions quickly while dribbling, and jump stop.

Equipment

- ✓ One basketball per player
- ✓ One portable basket per two players
- ✓ Tape or cones as markers (optional)
- ✓ Rubber band

Warm-Up (10 minutes)

Pairs—Partners practice shooting in the game Around the Key. They keep track of the number of baskets made.

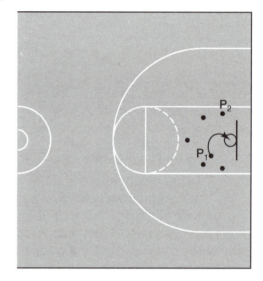

Fitness Circle (5 minutes)

Key Idea: Flexibility

Bring a rubber band and show children or have them visualize one. "This rubber band is like our muscles. When I pull it, it stretches; when I let go, it pulls back to its original shape." Show the action of a band—stretch it out and back; repeat, using a gentle, slow action. "Your muscles work the same way. When you reach and stretch, your muscles are stretching just like the rubber band. When your body comes back, your muscles go back to their original shape. Everyone slowly reach down to the floor with your arms and then bring your arms back up." Have children repeat three times. "Your leg muscles need to stretch because we use them a lot in basketball; it makes them more flexible. When muscles are flexible, it keeps them from getting hurt and makes the muscles feel good."

Practice 6

Game 1 (10 minutes)

Goal

Players dribble and drive to shoot.

Description

2 v 2, modified half-court game—If a team makes a basket, that team gets the ball again (gets a second turn). Designate the area (such as the lane) from which players must shoot to earn a point. Call modified double dribble and traveling violations. For example, a player can stop and start toward the basket three times before you call a double dribble violation, and a player can take four steps while not dribbling before you call a traveling violation. If a violation occurs, the team's opponent takes a turn.

Coach: How do you use the dribble in basketball?
Players: To get close to the basket to shoot, to beat your opponent.

Coach: How do you do that?
Players: You change direction.

Skill Practice (20 minutes)

1. Introduce, demonstrate, and explain how to start, stop, and change direction quickly while dribbling (see pages 116–117).
2. Have your players practice starting and stopping and changing direction quickly while dribbling.

Description

Individual—Players practice starting and stopping and changing directions quickly while dribbling, using the following activities:

- Dribble moving slowly at first, and then gradually increase speed.
- On a signal, quickly stop both moving and dribbling—jump stop.

☞ Demonstrate the whole skill first, and then break it down into parts.

☞ Focus on one idea at a time.

Practice 6 (cont'd)

- Dribble in general space. On the signal, stop quickly in a front-back stance, maintain the dribble, and then continue moving forward on the signal. To increase the challenge, pivot in another direction, and then continue moving.
- Move from one basket to the next by dribbling, and then jump stop and shoot. All shooting should be close to the basket (within two feet).

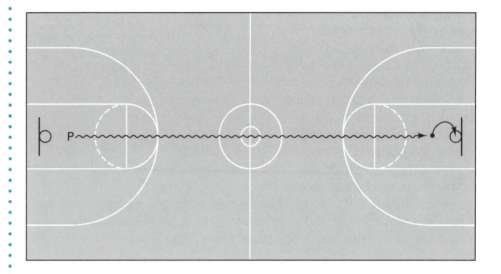

for jump stops
"Stay in a balanced position."
"Keep a front-back stance."
"Bend the knees."
"Lower the body."

Game 2 (10 minutes)

Goal

Players dribble and drive to shoot.

Description

Same as Game 1, except choose either 2 v 1 or 2 v 2. Rotate players accordingly so they all have a chance to play offense and defense.

Practice 6

Team Circle (5 minutes)

Key Idea: Responsibility

Gather children into a circle. You're in the middle of the circle with a ball. You'll try to dribble the ball out of the circle. The children will have two chances to keep the ball from escaping the circle. During one turn they'll use minimal effort, and during the second they'll use their maximum effort. "I am going to try to dribble the ball out of the circle. Everyone work together to keep the ball in the circle. Pretend that you are snails that can't get to the ball fast enough." Begin to dribble and try to get the ball out of the circle, reminding players that snails move slower. "This time move like busy bees that fly fast and keep moving." Repeat activity, encouraging players to be "busy bees." "When you try to be like busy bees, you're being responsible to your teammates."

Wrap-Up

Make summary comments about practice. Remind players of the next practice day and time and give them a sneak preview of that practice—keeping possession of the ball.

Variations

- Remember, changing the ball can make skill practice simpler or more challenging.
- To simplify the skill practice, limit the number of skill practice activities.

Practice 1

PURPOSE

To keep possession of the ball, focusing on increasing the proficiency of ballhandling and dribbling. The objective is for players to be able to handle a ball and dribble under control.

Equipment

- ☑ One basketball per player
- ☑ One portable basket per two players (if possible)
- ☑ Tape or cones as markers (optional)

Warm-Up (10 minutes)

Individual—Each player dribbles from one basket to the other, and then jump stops and shoots. All shooting should be close to the basket (within two feet).

Fitness Circle (5 minutes)

Key Idea: Muscular strength and endurance

Gather children in a group. Have a ball and show children the differences between a dribble with minimal effort and close to maximum effort. "Watch how the ball moves when I dribble it two different times." Show both dribbles to children. "Let's make a circle and you show me how you would dribble the ball. Show me a slow dribble; pretend you have a ball. Now step back two big steps and show me a fast dribble as you go across the circle." Highlight the ball going farther in the second dribble. "You can dribble the ball farther when the muscles in your arms are strong. The muscles in your arms get stronger when you practice dribbling."

Game 1 (10 minutes)

Goal

Players keep possession of the ball using a dribble.

Description

2 v 2, modified half-court game—Each player attempts to dribble and shoot at a basket (or target) while being guarded by an opponent. The offensive team must pass twice or more before shooting. Teams earn a point if they dribble and attempt a shot close to the basket (for example, in the lane).

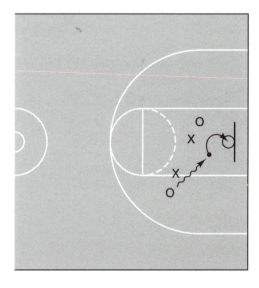

Practice 1

Designate the area (such as the lane) from which players must shoot to earn a point. Call modified double dribble and traveling violations. For example, a player can stop and start toward the basket three times before you call a double dribble violation, and a player can take four steps while not dribbling before you call a traveling violation. If a violation occurs, the team's opponent takes a turn.

Coach: What are the different ways that you have moved toward the basket (target) while dribbling?
Players: Dribbling fast or slow, changing direction, and stopping and starting.

Coach: How do you do that?
Players: Keep the ball low; change hands; keep the ball at my side; use my fingerpads; keep my eyes over the ball.

Skill Practice (20 minutes)

Description

Individual—Each player practices dribbling. Players can choose the size and weight of the ball they use. Have them try the following activities:

- Dribbling and changing the speed of movement (moving both fast and slow in general space).
- Dribbling while changing directions forward and back or right to left.
- Dribbling in different pathways:
  —Move in straight, curved, and zigzag pathways in general space.
  —Follow the straight lines on the gym floor.
  —Move in a straight pathway. Each time a player meets another person or hears your signal, he or she turns quickly to the right or left and continues dribbling.
  —Move throughout general space, quickly moving from side to side in a zigzag.

COACH's cues

"Use your fingerpads."
"Keep your eyes over the ball."
"Keep the ball low."
"Keep the ball at your side."

COACH's point

☞ You can review previous dribbling activities.

63

Practice 1 (cont'd)

Game 2 (10 minutes)

Goal

Players keep possession of the ball using a dribble.

Description

Same as Game 1, except choose either 2 v 1 or 2 v 2. Rotate players accordingly so they all have a chance to play offense and defense. Also, players earn one point for a shot attempt and one point for dribbling under control.

Team Circle (5 minutes)

Key Idea: Respect

Gather children into a group. "I'm going to ask you some questions about things I notice on this team. Tell me if you agree. Do you try to learn new skills at practice? Do you work hard to improve your skills? Do you help your teammates? Do you follow directions? Do you feel good about yourselves when you play a good game?" Listen to responses following each question. "Think about players who will be your opponents. What qualities or things do they have or do? Are they the same as you?" Listen for yes or no. "It's important to think of our opponents in the same way we think of ourselves. You respect yourself, and you should respect your opponents. They are a lot like you and are learning the same things."

Wrap-Up

Make summary comments about practice. Remind players of the next practice day and time and give them a sneak preview of that practice—dribbling under pressure.

Variations

To make the skill practice easier, use fewer activities.

Practice 8

Warm-Up (10 minutes)

Individual—Each player dribbles from one basket to the other, and then jump stops and shoots. All shooting should be close to the basket (within two feet).

Fitness Circle (5 minutes)

Key Idea: Training and conditioning

Gather children into a circle. "What will you do tonight after you eat dinner?" Wait for their responses. "At the end of the day what do you do?" Encourage children to discuss sleep. "Let's pretend you are at your homes, and you climb into bed to go to sleep. Everyone lie down. Now let's pretend it's morning and a new day. You don't have basketball practice today. Your body needs to move every day to stay in good physical condition for basketball. What should we do to move our bodies?" Wait for their responses. If a child suggests biking, walking, or swimming, and so on, have everyone pretend to do that activity. Then have them "sleep" again, wake up, and choose another physical activity idea.

Game 1 (10 minutes)

Goal

Players keep possession of the ball until they shoot.

Description

3 v 2, modified half-court game—Three players play offense and two players defend, then two offensive players must switch roles with the defensive players. Switch at least twice so all players get to play defense. Players earn a point if they keep possession of the ball (dribble with control) until they shoot or they attempt a shot close to the basket. Designate the area (such as the lane) from which players must shoot to earn a point. Call modified double dribble and traveling violations. For example, a player can stop and start toward the basket three times before you call a double dribble violation, and a player can take four steps while not dribbling before you call a traveling violation. If a violation occurs, the team's opponent takes a turn.

👉 PURPOSE

To keep possession of the ball, focusing on dribbling and protecting the ball. The objective is for players to be able to dribble under pressure.

Equipment

- ☑ One basketball per player
- ☑ One portable basket per two players (if possible)
- ☑ Tape or cones as markers (optional)

Practice 8 (cont'd)

Coach: What ways can you move to protect the basketball from your opponent when dribbling?
Players: Keep the ball on my side; keep the ball low; and change directions.

Skill Practice (20 minutes)

1. Introduce, demonstrate, and explain how to keep possession of the ball while dribbling (see pages 121–122).
2. Have players practice keeping possession of the ball while dribbling.

Description

Individual—Each player practices dribbling. Players choose the size and weight of the ball they use. At this point, you should provide players with situations in which they must dribble with either hand without looking at the ball. Set up obstacles so players can learn to vary the force of the bounce. Here are some examples:

- Dribble in different pathways:
  —Play follow-the-leader with a partner (followers are three feet behind).
  —Design strategies to outwit an imaginary opponent from baseline to baseline.

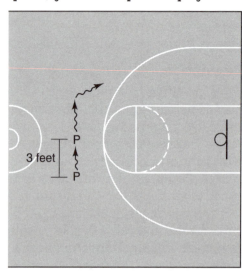

Practice 8

- Dribble around stationary obstacles. Set up cone markers three feet apart. Players try to dribble 60 seconds without bumping into the cones.

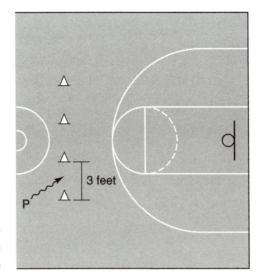

- Dribble around stationary players. Divide players into groups of five to six players. One player is the dribbler. The other players in the group become the obstacles and arrange themselves in a zigzag obstacle pattern down the floor. The players try to make the dribbler lose control of the ball. They can stretch and pivot, but cannot move from their spots; the defensive players cannot touch the ball or the dribbler. (When the player is ready, you can make this exercise more challenging by allowing the defensive players to touch the ball but not the dribbler.)

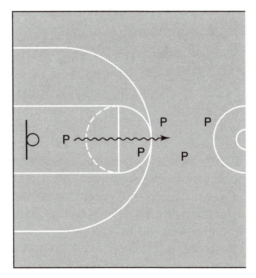

- Dribbling against an opponent. Match partners with similar skill levels. Partner 1 begins dribbling and moving toward the baseline while partner 2 plays cooperative defense. Increase the difficulty by moving to active defense. If partner 2 takes the ball away before 30 seconds are up, he or she gives it back; when 30 seconds are up, partners switch roles.

COACH's cues

"Keep your body between the obstacle and the ball."

"Keep the ball at your side."

Practice 8 (cont'd)

Game 2 (10 minutes)

Goal
Players keep possession of the ball until they shoot.

Description
Same as Game 1.

Team Circle (5 minutes)

Key Idea: Responsibility

Gather children into a group. Dump five to six balls out of a mesh ball bag, leaving them where they stop. "Pretend we just finished one activity in practice and we're getting ready to do something else. Everyone walk away from the balls and make a group circle." Pick up the balls, then go to the group. Dump balls out again. "Now come back and you pick up the balls, then go make a circle. Which way makes it faster for me to get to your circle?" Listen to their responses. "What do you think we should do with the balls?" Listen to their responses. Discuss picking up equipment before doing another activity. "We can have more fun and learn more when we work together. That is a shared responsibility between the coach and the players."

Wrap-Up
Make summary comments about practice. Remind players of the next practice day and time and give them a sneak preview of that practice—defending an opponent.

☞ Find success in everything players attempt. Use the KIS principle: (Keep it successful!).

Variations

- When working with the players on dribbling, you can vary the activity depending on the developmental needs of the player. You can establish an accountability check, in which you or a player's peer witnesses a demonstration of proficiency for each activity.
- To simplify the skill practice, limit the number of skill practice activities.

Practice 9

Warm-Up (10 minutes)

Pairs—Partner 1 dribbles the ball 8 to 10 times and then passes it to partner 2. Partner 2 starts dribbling the ball forward and then passes it back to partner 1. The partners continue to dribble and pass from one end of the gym to the other (see the figure on page 52).

Fitness Circle (5 minutes)

Key Idea: Muscular strength and endurance

Have children spread out in a group. "Put your hand on the front of your thigh, then lift your leg up and set it down. Did you feel the muscle get tight when you lifted it up and then relax when you set it down? Try it again five times." Assist players if needed. "Muscles tighten or contract when you move. You use the thigh muscles or quadriceps when you play basketball. The more you practice, the stronger your thigh or quadriceps muscles will get. That's called improving your muscular strength."

PURPOSE

To defend your own space, focusing on basic defensive technique. The objective is for players to be able to defend an opponent.

Equipment

- ✓ One basketball per player (if possible)
- ✓ One portable basket per two players (if possible)
- ✓ Tape or cones as markers (optional)

Game 1 (10 minutes)

Goal

Players learn basic defensive technique.

Description

3 v 3, short-court game—Defensive players earn a point when they take the ball away. Limit offensive players to dribbling three times or less before passing. Call modified double dribble and traveling violations. For example, a player can stop and start toward the basket three times before you call a double dribble violation,

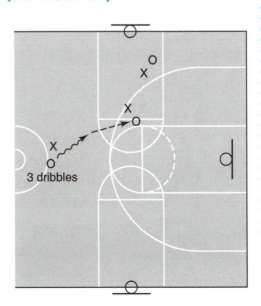
3 dribbles

Practice 9 (cont'd)

and a player can take four steps without dribbling before you call a traveling violation. If a violation occurs, the player's opponent takes a turn. Starting with this game, call fouls as violations. The defender can touch the ball, but he or she cannot touch the opponent. If a violation occurs, the opponent gets the ball.

Coach: What do you do when you are playing defense?
Players: Try to get the ball and protect the basket.

Coach: How do you defend your basket?
Players: Play the person with the ball and try to get the ball.

Skill Practice (15 minutes)

1. Introduce, demonstrate, and explain how to defend against an opponent (see pages 126–129).
2. Have your players practice defending against an opponent.

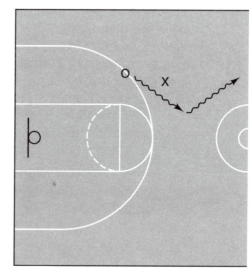

Description

Pairs—Match players of similar skill. The defensive player moves in a defensive position in front of the offensive player, who dribbles slowly, then gradually faster in a zigzag pathway. Then have players perform the same exercise and switch roles. Have players change partners every three to five minutes.

☞ Try not to get caught up in the details of defense. More will come later when players are more developmentally ready. As we know, defense is hard work!

COACH's cues

for basic defensive position

"Keep the knees bent."
"Keep your body low."
"Put one hand up, one hand down."
"Keep a wide stance."

for playing defense

"See the ball, not the opponent."
"Play the ball." (Players should focus on the ball, not the person dribbling it.)

Practice 9

Game 2 (15 minutes)

Goal

Players will use basic defense in a game.

Description

Same as Game 1, except choose either 1 v 3, 2 v 3, or 3 v 3. Rotate players accordingly so they all have a chance to play offense and defense.

Team Circle (5 minutes)

Key Idea: Respect

Gather children into a single-file line near two cones about 10 feet apart. "I am going to walk down the line two times. Remember how it feels each time I pass you." Walk down the line and nod to each player. Repeat, but this time tell each player "great game" or "nice play today" and shake his or her hand. "Which time that I passed you made you feel better?" Ask children to stand near a cone that represents their choice. "Shaking hands and saying 'good game' are important traditions that show we appreciate our opponents' efforts in a game. It shows respect for your opponents." Divide team in half and have them practice an end of game "respect ritual."

Wrap-Up

Make summary comments about practice. Remind players of the next practice day and time and give them a sneak preview of that practice— passing and receiving and supporting the teammate with the ball.

Variations

- To simplify skill practices, modify the ball to meet players' needs. To simplify games, modify the size and height of the basket or target.
- To increase the challenge during skill practices, use a larger ball. To increase the challenge during games, modify the size and height of the basket or target and limit rule modifications.

71

Practice 10

PURPOSE

To play a 3 v 3 game, focusing on keeping possession of the ball. The objective is for players to be able to pass and receive and to support teammates with the ball.

Equipment

- ✓ One basketball per player (if possible)
- ✓ One portable basket per two players (if possible)
- ✓ Tape or cones as markers (optional)

Warm-Up (10 minutes)

Pairs—The defensive player moves in a defensive position in front of the offensive player, who is dribbling slowly and then gradually dribbles faster in a zigzag pathway. The offensive player changes speed and directions. The players move down the length of floor, and then switch roles (see the figure on page 70).

Fitness Circle (5 minutes)

Key Idea: Healthy habits

Gather children into a group. "When I say 'Go!' we all will run as fast as we can, without bumping into each other, staying in this area." Mark boundary areas for children. "Ready, go!" Have children run for about a minute or until fatigued. "You had enough energy to run. But when you don't take care of your body, you can get tired much faster playing basketball. I am going to say a habit and you shout if it is healthy or unhealthy." Examples: taking drugs, smoking, brushing teeth, drinking plenty of water, getting plenty of sleep/rest, eating a variety of foods. "Can you think of any others? Healthy or unhealthy?"

Game 1 (10 minutes)

Goal

Groups of three players will play as opposing teams.

Description

3 v 3, short-court game (see the figure on page 69)—Limit players to dribbling three times or less before passing (you can modify the number of dribbles as necessary). Call modified double dribble and traveling violations. For example, a player can stop and start toward the basket three times before you call a double dribble violation, and a player can take four steps without dribbling the ball before you call a traveling violation. If a violation occurs, the team's opponent takes a turn. Also call modified foul violations. This allows the defender to touch the ball, but not the opponent. If a violation occurs, the opponent gets the ball.

Practice 10

Coach: What do you have to do to work as a team?
Players: You have to help each other out and support your teammate.

Coach: How do you help each other out?
Players: You get ready to receive a pass and move around.

Skill Practice (15 minutes)

1. Introduce, demonstrate, and explain how to dribble and pass in a game situation (see pages 119–122).
2. Have your students practice dribbling and passing in a game situation.

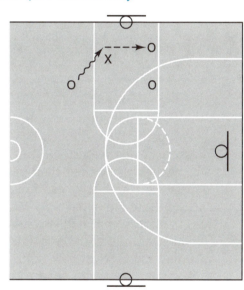

Description

Groups of four—Three players dribble and pass while the fourth player tries to steal the ball. Rotate the player trying to steal the ball every two minutes. This is a no-contact game. Limit the space used for the game to half of a short court.

COACH's cue

"Change directions, speed, and pathways."

COACH's point

☞ The key in this practice is to get the players to move to an open space.

73

Practice 10 (cont'd)

Game 2 (15 minutes)

Goal

Groups of players will play as opposing teams.

Description

Same as Game 1, except choose either 2 v 3 or 3 v 3. Rotate players accordingly so they all have a chance to play offense and defense.

Team Circle (5 minutes)

Key Idea: Keeping perspective

Gather children into a group near two cones about 10 feet apart. "What did you most enjoy learning about in basketball this season?" Listen to their responses. "Players who thought they tried their best to learn, stand by this cone. Players who think they had fun this season, stand by this one. Both of those are important. You should try your best and have fun no matter what happens during the season. The most important thing in basketball is to have fun playing with friends and to learn new skills. I think you all did that! Next year is another chance to have fun and make new friends!"

Wrap-Up

Make summary comments about what players learned over the season. Encourage players to come back next year.

Variations

- To increase the challenge during the skill practice, have players play 2 v 1.
- To increase the challenge during games, limit the rules modifications.

chapter 7

Practice Plans for Six- to Seven-Year-Olds

This chapter contains 10 practice plans to use with your six- to seven-year-old YMCA Rookies basketball players. Before we get to those, though, we'll explain how the YMCA Rookies program modifies basketball and give you a quick review of what's in the lesson plans and how you should use them.

Game Modifications

All games for six- to seven-year-olds will be played on a half-court or short courts (see figure 7.1), using modified game rules (see chapter 9 for basketball rules). Because young players have to learn about violations (such as forgetting to dribble the ball while moving) and fouls (illegal contact with an opposing player) gradually, the rules for YMCA Rookies basketball have the following modifications:

- Players are to follow a self-space rule, which has three parts:
  - Players may not block shots or touch the ball when the ballhandler is holding the ball, but they may steal the ball when it is passed or dribbled.

— Defending players may not intentionally get in the path of an offensive player to take a defensive charge.

— Defending players may not undercut an offensive player who is shooting an uncontested layup. This rule minimizes fouls and controls playing defense.

- Only player-to-player defense is used, not zones.
- No shot clock or scoreboard is used.
- Players are to follow a keep control rule, which says that players must keep physical control of their bodies and the ball. No rough play is allowed.
- All players must be good sports and show respect. Players who show unsporting conduct should be penalized by being removed from the game for a time.

Games may be played in one of three ways:

1. **Modified half-court games.** Individual players (1 v 1) or teams (2 v 1, 2 v 2, 3 v 2, or 3 v 3) take turns trying to score, and then switch roles from offense to defense or vice versa.

2. **Short-court games.** Short-court games require baskets at the sides of a regular basketball court. Using a short court is best for developing skills in younger players.

3. **Regular half-court games.** If an offensive player or team rebounds the ball, that individual or team can shoot again. If the defensive player or team rebounds the ball, that player or team must restart at the top of the key.

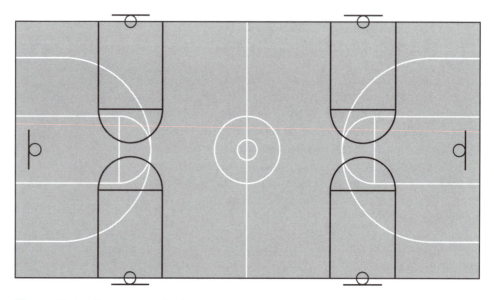

Figure 7.1 Crosscourt playing area.

During game play be sure to rotate opponents. You can arrange several short games (three to five minutes) and rotate opponents at the beginning of each new game. Remember that changing opponents changes the game. Have no more than seven players to a team.

Having the right amount and type of equipment is critical to the success of the YMCA Rookies program. All aspects of the game must be modified for this level of play. Table 7.1 gives you some examples.

To help players learn, you can work with players in two ways:

- Teach by invitation. Adjust for individual differences in players by inviting the players to decide some of the parameters of the practice situation themselves, such as choosing the size of the ball.
- Vary the parameters of the practice yourself in order to make play easier or more challenging for individuals or small groups.

Using either strategy allows players to succeed while being challenged; play isn't too hard or too easy.

To simplify the game or to increase the challenge for players, try the following:

- Change the size and weight of the ball.
- Change the size and height of the basket.
- Give players timed goals, and then increase or decrease the interval or duration.
- Give players trial goals, and then increase or decrease the number of times the skill must be done successfully.

TABLE 7.1

Modified Factors in Basketball

Factors	YMCA Rookies basketball
Size and weight of ball	Junior #5
Height of basket	6 feet—bushel baskets or wash baskets hung on the walls work well
Size of basket	Large to regulation
Number of players	Small sided (1 v 1, 2 v 1, 2 v 2, 3 v 2, 3 v 3)
Court size	Half-court, short court
Number of players per team	7

In the YMCA Rookies basketball program, players focus on skills related to offense. Defensive skills are important, but if those skills are introduced too soon, players may have difficulty developing offensive skills, especially if their peers play defense aggressively. Introduce defensive skills after players have developed some proficiency with off- and on-the-ball skills. Rather than eliminating defense, we recommend that you control defensive play by using two levels of involvement:

1. **Cooperative defense (cold).** The player assumes a defensive posture two arm lengths from the opponent and is relatively passive.

2. **Active defense (warm).** The player assumes a defensive posture about one and a half arm lengths from the opponent, has active hands and feet, but makes no attempts to intercept the ball.

Players who are four- to five-years-old should use cooperative defense; players who are six- to seven-years-old start out using cooperative defense and, after Practice 5, move to active defense.

Here are some other ways to make practice games simpler or more challenging:

- Equally increase or decrease the number of players suggested (for example, if we suggest playing 2 v 2, make it simpler by playing 1 v 1, or make it more challenging by playing 3 v 3).
- Begin with *no* defense.
- Add an extra offensive player to make it easier for the offense (for example, 3 v 2 instead of 2 v 2).
- Add an extra defender to make it harder on the offense (for example, 2 v 3 instead of 3 v 3) once players have acquired the skills they need to be successful.
- Perform the skill or game at a slower than normal pace to make it simpler.
- Increase or decrease the number of passes you require before the offense can attempt a shot.

All these suggested modifications will help your YMCA Rookies players develop their basketball skills at a level at which they can succeed. As they become more skilled, the game rules will become more like those of the official game. YMCA Rookies practices will give your players a good foundation to build on as they grow.

Practice Plan Organization

Each plan contains the following sections:

- Purpose
- Equipment

- Practice Plan
- Coach's Point
- Variations

Purpose focuses on what you want to teach your players during that practice; it is your main theme for the day. *Equipment* notes what you'll need on hand for that practice. We'll address the *Practice Plan* in depth in just a moment. The *Coach's Point* lists helpful reminders for you, points of emphasis to most effectively conduct the practice. We include *Variations* to games at the end of each plan, providing you with modifications to keep skill practices and games fun and interesting and to help players of varying skill levels.

The Practice Plan section outlines what you will do during each practice session. It consists of these elements:

- Warm-up
- Fitness Circle
- Game 1
- Skill Practices and Games
- Team Circle and Wrap-Up

You'll begin each session with 5- to 10-minute warm-up activities. (Note: All times given in the practice plans are approximate.) This warm-up will be followed by five minutes of the Fitness Circle, during which you briefly talk with players about an idea that relates to health or fitness. Then, in Game 1, you'll be working on the first two steps of the four-step process for teaching basketball: having players play a modified basketball game and helping them discover what they need to do. The game will be designed to focus players' attention on a particular aspect of basketball. Start the game but, when it's clear that the players are having trouble achieving the goal of the game, stop the game and ask questions and get answers similar to those shown in the plans. The questions and answers will help the players see what skills they need to solve tactical problems in the game.

The third part of the three-step process is teaching the skills identified in Game 1 through the skill practices. In each skill practice, you'll use the IDEA approach, which means you do the following actions:

I Introduce the skill.

D Demonstrate the skill.

E Explain the skill.

A Attend to players practicing the skill.

Chapter 8 contains descriptions of all the skills, so we give you a page reference in the skill practices to guide you to the appropriate description. The introduction, demonstration, and explanation should be very brief to fit young children's short attention spans. Then, as the players practice, you will attend to individual children and guide them with teaching cues or further demonstration.

Coaching YMCA Rookies Basketball

After the skill practices, you will have the children play another game to finish the four-step process. This lets them use the skills they just learned and helps them understand how to utilize those skills in the context of a game. Note that in Game 1, when players are being introduced to a new tactic or skill, they usually will play an even-sided game (such as 3 v 3). This allows them to encounter the challenges they will face in executing the tactic or skill. Then, in most Game 2s, they play lopsided games (such as 3 v 1 or 3 v 2) to increase their chances of experiencing success and beginning to master the new tactic or skill. However, if your players are showing proficiency with the new tactic or skill, you can use even-sided games in Game 2. The choice is yours; for more on this issue, see chapter 4.

Each practice plan concludes with a Team Circle, which focuses on character development. You will take about five minutes to talk to your players about some aspect of basketball that relates to one of the four core values: caring, honesty, respect, and responsibility. Following this, you'll wrap up the practice with a reminder of the next practice day and time and a preview of what will be taught in the next practice session.

Note that Fitness and Team Circle times are meant to be true discussions, not lectures where you do all the talking and the players do all the listening. Ask the questions provided and wait for your players to respond. Don't feed them the answers that we provide; these answers are only meant to help you guide the discussion. Your role is as much to ask questions and get players to respond as it is to dole out information.

The plans in this chapter, combined with the information in the rest of this book, should give you what you need to lead practices. Just remember to be patient and caring as you work on skills. Different children will progress at different rates, and it's more important that they learn the sport in a positive way than it is that they learn quickly.

Key to Diagrams

△ = Cone

• = Marked "spot" on court

■ = Block

---▶ = Pass

──▶ = Run

∿▶ = Dribble

P = Player or partner

⤹ = Shoot

O = Offensive player

X = Defensive player

S = Supporting player

Practice 1

Warm-Up (10 minutes)

Begin each practice with 5 to 10 minutes of warm-up activities to get players loosened up and ready to go.

Individual—Players should stand apart from each other (allow 15 seconds for them to move to their own space); on the signal, players begin dribbling in general space without losing control. Players should stop and catch the ball quickly on a signal. Repeat this activity three times in short intervals (20, 30, and 45 seconds).

Fitness Circle (5 minutes)

Following the warm-up, gather the players and briefly discuss the fitness concept for that practice.

Key Idea: General fitness

"In basketball, running makes our hearts beat faster and our leg muscles stronger. Spread out into your own space. Everyone run in place and I will pass the ball to some of you. If you get the ball, pass it back to me and keep running!" Continue for about 30 seconds. "Playing basketball improves our physical conditioning or fitness. We get better at running, jumping, and dribbling the ball, and we can keep going longer before we get too tired. How can I keep from getting too tired when I'm running?" Pacing. "How about dribbling?" Practice at home. "It is also important to take a rest when you need one and to drink water during practice and at home. We will talk more about the different areas of fitness in our Fitness Circles throughout the season."

Game 1 (10 minutes)

Following the Fitness Circle, get the kids playing a game. After letting the players play a while, interrupt the game for a time of questions and answers—with YOU asking the questions and your PLAYERS providing the answers (about what the goal of the game was and what skills and tactics they needed to perform to succeed in the game). For many games, we provide diagrams or figures showing how the game is played. We also often provide "coach's points" for you to pass along to your players during the games.

☞ PURPOSE

To keep possession of the ball, focusing on increasing the proficiency of ballhandling and dribbling. The objective is for players to be able to handle the ball and dribble under control.

Equipment

- ☑ One basketball per player
- ☑ One portable basket per two players
- ☑ Tape or cones as markers (optional)

Practice 1 (cont'd)

COACH's point

☞ Spend time helping players understand how to play a modified half-court game. The games are more cooperative than competitive, limiting players' focus to boundaries, starting and restarting game play, and keeping control. Be flexible regarding all violations (such as double dribble or traveling); however, you will need a keep control rule. For example, if a player just picks up the ball and starts running with it without dribbling, that would be out of control. Teach cooperative (cold) defense to the players.

Goal
Players dribble and drive during a 1 v 1 game.

Description
1 v 1, modified half-court game—Explain how to start and restart the game. Each player takes a turn driving to the basket. His or her opponent plays cooperative defense. Players earn a point for keeping possession and attempting a shot.

You'll follow Game 1 with a Skill Practice, during which you'll introduce, demonstrate, and explain a skill or tactic, and then attend to your players as they practice it. The question-and-answer session, in which your players tell YOU what skills and tactics they needed to be successful in the game, leads directly to the Skill Practice. We often provide coaching points with the Skill Practices; pass these points along to your players. We also provide "coach's cues"—phrases to help your players focus on the task at hand—during many Skill Practices and Games.

Coach: What is the goal of the game?
Players: To put the ball in the basket, to score a basket.

Coach: What are different ways that you can move toward the basket (target) while dribbling?
Players: You can dribble fast or slow, change direction, or stop and start.

Coach: How do you do that? (This question is to see what players know about dribbling.)
Players: You keep the ball low, change hands, keep the ball at your side, use the fingerpads, and keep your eyes over the ball.

Skill Practice (20 minutes)

1. Introduce, demonstrate, and explain how to handle the ball and dribble (see pages 121–122).
2. Have players practice ballhandling and dribbling.

Description
Individual—Each player practices dribbling. Players can choose the size and weight of the ball they use. At this point, you should provide

Practice 1

players with situations in which they must dribble with either hand, without looking at the ball. Set up obstacles so players can learn to vary the force of the bounce. Here are some examples:

- Dribbling and changing the speed of movement (moving both fast and slow in general space).
- Dribbling while changing directions forward and back or right to left.
- Dribbling in different pathways:
  —Move in straight, curved, and zigzag pathways in general space.
  —Follow the straight lines on the gym floor.
  —Move in a straight pathway. Each time a player meets another person or hears your signal, he or she turns quickly to the right or left and continues dribbling.
  —Move in a series of curved pathways. If the player curves to the left, he or she must dribble with the right hand; if the player curves to the right, he or she must dribble with the left hand. The player must always keep the ball on the outside of the curve.
- Move throughout general space, quickly moving from side to side in a zigzag.

COACH's cues

"Use your fingerpads."
"Keep your eyes over the ball."
"Keep the ball low."
"Keep the ball at your side."

Game 2 (10 minutes)

Goal
Players dribble and drive.

Description
Same as Game 1.

Practice 1 (cont'd)

Team Circle (5 minutes)

Conclude practice by gathering your players and discussing a character development concept. These aren't lectures; you want your players' active participation in these discussions. Following the discussions, wrap up the practice with a few comments (which in most practices are bulleted items).

Key Idea: Four core values

Gather children into a circle with one ball. "Everyone hand the ball to the one next to you until it makes it around the whole circle." After the ball has gone around the circle one time, have it passed to you. "We play basketball to be more healthy and fit, but it also teaches us to become good teammates and good people. This season we will talk about four qualities of a good person and teammate: *caring, honesty, respect,* and *responsibility.* Our team needs to have all of these qualities in our practices and games. Remember—we can't be a team without each of you doing your part. Let's pass the ball to each other and say one of the care values before you pass. This will help you remember to use all four of the qualities so we can work together."

Wrap-Up

Make summary comments about practice. Remind players of the next practice day and time and give them a sneak preview of that practice—passing and receiving the basketball.

Variations

- When working with the players on dribbling, you can vary the activity depending on the developmental needs of the player.
- You can review previous dribbling activities. For example, use the time while players are arriving to set up stations that review activities from the program for four- and five-year-olds. Set up four to six skill practice stations at different places in your gym. Then divide your team into small groups (from two to three players) and have each group spend 20 to 30 seconds at each station, and then take 10 seconds to rotate to the next station. Players leave the equipment at each station; use boxes or hoops as a place to deposit the balls.

Practice 2

Warm-Up (10 minutes)

Individual or group—Players practice dribbling in the following ways either individually, in a small group, or under your direction:

- Dribbling and changing speed of travel (travel both fast and slow in general space).
- Dribbling while changing directions (forward and backward, right to left).
- Dribbling in straight, curved, and zigzag pathways.

☞ PURPOSE

To keep possession of the ball, focusing on passing and dribbling with a partner. The objective is for players to be able to pass and receive the basketball.

Equipment

- ✓ One basketball per player (if possible)
- ✓ One portable basket per two players (if possible)
- ✓ Tape or cones as markers (optional)
- ✓ Rubber band (optional)

Fitness Circle (5 minutes)

Key Idea: Flexibility

Bring a rubber band and show it to the children or have them visualize one. "This rubber band is like our muscles. Can you tell me why?" Listen for children's responses—stretches when pulled, goes back to original shape, and so on. Demonstrate band movement. "Your muscles work the same way. When you reach and stretch, your muscles stretch just like the rubber band. When your body comes back, your muscles go back to their original shape. Everyone reach down to the floor with your arms slowly and then bring your arms back up." Have children repeat three times. "Your leg muscles need to stretch because we use them the most in basketball. It makes them more flexible. When muscles are flexible, it keeps them from getting hurt and makes the muscles feel good."

Game 1 (10 minutes)

Goal

Pairs of players will play as a team.

Description

2 v 1, modified half-court game—Two players become partners and play against one defensive player, then one partner must switch roles with the defensive player. Switch at least twice so all players get to play defense. A team earns a point when they have one completed pass

Practice 2 (cont'd)

before the shot. Limit them to dribbling three times or less before passing. Call modified traveling violations. For example, a player can take three steps without dribbling the ball before you call a traveling violation.

Explain to players that they are expected to be good sports and to show respect to other players. If a player shows unsporting conduct, he or she will be removed from the game for a few minutes.

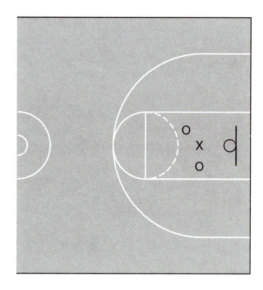

Coach: What is the goal of the game?
Players: To keep the ball to score; to dribble and pass to score.

Coach: What do you have to do to be successful at passing?
Players: You have to catch the ball and pass it right to your teammate.

Coach: What types of passes are there? (This question is to see how much players know about passing.)
Players: The bounce pass and chest pass (see page 120).

Coach: How do you play as a team?
Players: You work together and talk to each other.

Skill Practice (20 minutes)

1. Introduce, demonstrate, and explain how to dribble and pass to a partner (see pages 119–122).
2. Have your players practice dribbling and passing to a partner.

Description

Pairs—Partner 1 dribbles 8 to 10 times and then passes to partner 2 (see the figure on page 52). Partner 2 starts dribbling forward and then passes back to partner 1. The partners continue to dribble and pass to each other from one end of the gym to the other. They should try bounce and chest passes. The object is to make four successful passes in a row.

Game 2 (15 minutes)

Goal

Players will pass and receive in a game.

Description

Same as Game 1, except that if a team makes a basket, they get the ball again (two turns only).

☞ Encourage players to move when they are dribbling.

☞ Remind passers to pass a little in front of their partners.

☞ If you find that you have to spend time with basic passing and receiving skills, return to Practice 3 for the four- to five-year-olds (in chapter 6) for review.

Practice 2

COACH's cues

"If you have the ball, you must dribble to move."
"Pass on the move."
"Control the ball."
"Lead your partner."

for receiving

"Target the hands."
"Keep your eyes on the ball."
"Reach for the ball."
"Pull the ball in."

for passing

"Put your hands on the sides of the ball, thumbs pointing to each other."
"Step forward with your preferred foot."
"Push the ball forward at chest level, elbows out, and snap it."
(After the pass) "Move thumbs down, backs of your hands facing each other, and move your weight forward."

Team Circle (5 minutes)

Key Idea: Responsibility

Gather children into a group. "When you come to practice, you should do three things: (1) Be ready to play. (2) Learn and improve your skills and work with others. (3) Have fun. I'm going to give you a way to remember these three things. It's called a 'team motto.' Our team motto is *Play hard, play fair, and have fun!* Let's say it together out loud. That's great. Be sure to remember our team motto and put it into practice."

Wrap-Up

Make summary comments about practice. Remind players of the next practice day and time and give them a sneak preview of that practice—shooting the ball.

Practice 3

☞ PURPOSE

To attack the basket, focusing on shooting close to the basket. The objective is for players to be able to shoot using basic technique.

Equipment

- ☑ One basketball per player (if possible)
- ☑ One portable basket per two players (if possible)
- ☑ Tape or cones as markers (optional)

Warm-Up (10 minutes)

Choose one of these two activities:

1. Individual—Players dribble around cones spaced three feet apart. They try to dribble 60 seconds without bumping into any cones.
2. Pairs—Players pair up with partners of similar skill. Partner 1 dribbles toward the baseline while partner 2 plays cooperative defense. You can increase the difficulty by moving to active defense.

Fitness Circle (5 minutes)

Key Idea: Cardiorespiratory fitness

Gather children into a group. "Everyone hold one hand up and make a fist. Squeeze your fist tightly, then let go. Keep tightening and letting go." Children continue for 10 counts. "Your heart is a special muscle that tightens and relaxes just like your fist is doing. Your heart is about the size of your fist. Every time it tightens, or beats, it pumps blood all over your body. When you play basketball, your heart beats faster and you breathe faster. Run in place with high knees. Feel your lungs and feel your heart beating by placing your hands over your chest. Count how many times your heart beats." Time for 15 seconds. Ask players the number they counted. "Running helps you improve your cardiorespiratory fitness—the heart and lungs working together to get blood to your whole body."

Game 1 (10 minutes)

Goal

Players shoot close to the basket.

Description

2 v 1, modified half-court game—Two players become partners and play against one defensive player, then one partner must switch roles with the defensive player. Switch at least twice so all players get to play

Practice 3

defense. Teams earn one point if the ball touches the backboard or rim on the shot and two points if the ball goes into the basket. Call modified double dribble and traveling violations. For example, a player can stop and start toward the basket twice before you call a double dribble violation, and a player can take three steps without dribbling the ball before you call a traveling violation.

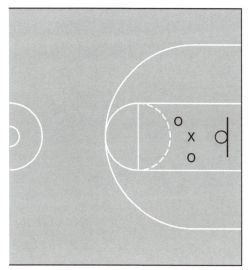

Coach: What is the goal of this game?
Players: The goal is to shoot at the basket and score points.

Coach: How do you do that?
Players: You shoot close to the basket.

Skill Practice (20 minutes)

1. Introduce, demonstrate, and explain how to shoot baskets with a set shot (see page 122–125).
2. Have your players practice shooting baskets with a set shot.

Description

Individual or pairs—Players practice shooting either individually or in pairs in a game of Around the Key (see the figure on page 56). For this game, mark shooting spots with tape in an arc around the basket (inside the key). All shots should be close to the basket. Each player moves from spot to spot in order, shooting from each spot. If pairs are playing, player 2 gets the rebound and passes the ball back to player 1. The key to success will be the size and weight of the ball the player uses as well as the height and size of the basket or target. Players should count the number of baskets made or "high five" their partners when those partners score a basket.

Game 2 (10 minutes)

Goal

Players keep possession in order to score.

Description

Same as Game 1.

Practice 3 (cont'd)

COACH's cues

"Keep hands apart on the ball."
"Only fingers touch the ball."
"Keep palms up."
"Point elbows toward the basket."
"Flip your wrist and wave good-bye." (The hand follows through after the shot.)

Variations

To simplify the skill practice, have players shoot close to the basket. To increase the challenge, increase the distance from the basket.

Team Circle (5 minutes)

Key Idea: Responsibility

Gather children into a group between two cones about 10 feet apart. Stand in the middle of the circle with a ball. "I am going to show you two different ways to handle the same situation. Think about which is the best way to handle this." Choose a player to receive a pass from you. Make a bad pass and then stomp angrily away from the group. Retrieve the ball and make another bad pass. This time, run to get the ball and make a pass that goes directly to the player. "If you think the first response is the way to handle making a bad pass, stand next to this cone. If you think the second way is better, stand next to this one." Ask players to explain their choices. "It's important to be a good sport in basketball." Highlight how and why. "That's being responsible to your teammates."

Wrap-Up

Make summary comments about practice. Remind players of the next practice day and time and give them a sneak preview of that practice—driving and dribbling to shoot.

COACH's point

☞ Demonstration is important; a picture is worth a thousand words.

☞ Although coaching cues are an important part of learning, you should limit the number of coaching cues you provide players to two to three at a time.

Practice 4

Warm-Up (10 minutes)

Pairs—Players practice shooting in a game of Around the Key. Use tape to mark shooting spots. Players should take all shots close to the basket (see the figure on page 56).

Fitness Circle (5 minutes)

Key Idea: Cardiorespiratory fitness

Gather children in a group. "Everyone put your hand up in the front of you and make a fist. What did we pretend our fist was at the last practice?" Wait for response—should be the heart. "What do our hearts do?" Wait for responses—pump blood. "Everybody open and close your fist. Put your hand over your chest and feel what is happening. Now, let's run to the hoop and back. Will our hearts beat faster or slower?" Listen to responses—should be faster. "Put your hand over your chest. Is your heart beating faster or slower? Are your lungs breathing faster or slower? When we run during basketball, the heart beats faster just like the fist opening and closing, and the lungs breathe faster. They slow down when we slow down. Making your heart beat faster helps to improve your cardiorespiratory fitness."

👉 PURPOSE

To keep possession of the ball and to attack the basket, focusing on driving and dribbling to shoot. The objective is for players to be able to start and stop, change directions quickly while dribbling, and jump stop.

Equipment

- ✓ One basketball per player (if possible)
- ✓ One portable basket per two players (if possible)
- ✓ Tape or cones as markers (optional)

Game 1 (10 minutes)

Goal

Players will use the dribble to drive and score.

Description

2 v 2, modified half-court game (see the figure on page 55)—Players earn a point if they use five dribbles or less before shooting. Remind players that even though they are playing as a team, they should also attempt to dribble and drive to the basket. Call modified double dribble and traveling violations. For example, a player can stop and start toward the basket twice before you call a double dribble violation, and a player can take three steps without dribbling the ball before you call a traveling violation.

Practice 4 (cont'd)

Coach: How do you use the dribble in basketball?
Players: To get close to the basket to shoot, to beat your opponent.

Coach: How do you do that?
Players: You change direction, speed, or pathways.

Skill Practice (20 minutes)

1. Introduce, demonstrate, and explain how to start and stop and change direction quickly while dribbling (see pages 116–117).
2. Have players practice starting and stopping and changing direction quickly while dribbling.

Description

Individual—Players practice starting and stopping and changing directions quickly while dribbling, using the following activities:

- Dribble moving slowly at first, and then gradually increase speed.
- On a signal, quickly stop both moving and dribbling—jump stop.
- Dribble in general space. On a signal, stop quickly in a front-back stance, maintain the dribble, and then continue moving forward on the signal. To increase the challenge, pivot in another direction, and then continue moving.
- Move from one basket to the next by dribbling, and then jump stop and shoot. All shooting should be close to the basket. Jump shots should be taken within two feet of the basket (see the figure on page 60).

COACH's cues

for dribbling
"Use your fingerpads."
"Keep your eyes over the ball."
"Keep the ball low."
"Keep the ball at your side."

for a jump stop
"Stay in a balanced position."
"Keep a front-back stance."
"Bend your knees."
"Lower your body."

Practice 4

Game 2 (10 minutes)

Goal

Players will use the dribble to drive and score.

Description

Same as Game 1, except choose either 2 v 1 or 2 v 2, depending on the skill proficiency of your players. Rotate players accordingly so they all have a chance to play offense and defense. (See chapter 4 for more on the use of lopsided games.) Also, if a team makes a basket, it gets the ball again (second turn only).

Team Circle (5 minutes)

Key Idea: Honesty

Gather children into a group near two cones about 10 feet apart. "What is a foul?" Listen to their responses. Choose a player to help demonstrate responses (include pushing, bumping players, and tripping). "Should you admit to a foul if no one sees it? Those who think yes, stand at this cone. Those who think no, stand at this one." Wait for children to choose. "When you know you've fouled, you should raise your hand. You should never take unfair advantage of other players. Can you think of other ways honesty is practiced on the court?" Listen to responses and discuss. "All of those show honesty."

Wrap-Up

Make summary comments about practice. Remind players of the next practice day and time and give them a sneak preview of that practice—dribbling under pressure.

COACH's point

☞ Remember to use your coaching cues; these short, catchy phrases call the players' attention to key components to improve performance.

Variations

Remember to simplify the skill practice or game or increase its challenge by using the suggestions at the beginning of this chapter.

93

Practice 5

👉 PURPOSE

To keep possession of the ball, focusing on dribbling and protecting the ball. The objective is for players to be able to dribble under pressure.

Equipment

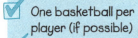 One basketball per player (if possible)

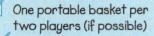 One portable basket per two players (if possible)

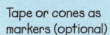 Tape or cones as markers (optional)

Warm-Up (10 minutes)

Individual—Players dribble from one basket to the next, and then jump stop and shoot. All shooting should be close to the basket. Jump shots should be taken within two feet of the basket (see the figure on page 60).

Fitness Circle (5 minutes)

Key Idea: Cardiorespiratory fitness

Gather children in a group. "Everyone find their own space. Put your fist up in front of you. We pretend our fist is our..." wait for response—heart. "The heart does what things?" Wait for response—pumps blood and beats faster when we run or move faster. "When I say 'Go!' run in your own space and make your fist open and close faster at the same time. When I say 'Stop!', stop as fast as you can." Begin activity. "When you run, your heart beats faster. Every time your heart beats faster, it gets stronger because it is a muscle. Muscles get stronger when you use them. Basketball is a great way to keep your heart healthy and strong and improve your cardiorespiratory fitness."

Game 1 (10 minutes)

Goal

Players keep possession in order to score.

Description

2 v 2, modified half-court game (see the figure on page 55)—A player scores a point for keeping possession and attempting a shot. Opponents play cooperative defense. If a team makes a basket, it gets the ball again (two turns only).

Call modified double dribble and traveling violations. For example, a player can stop and start toward the basket twice before you call a double dribble violation, and a player can take three steps without dribbling the ball before you call a traveling violation.

Practice 5

Coach: What ways can you move to protect the basketball from your opponent when dribbling?
Players: Keep the ball on my side; keep the ball low; change directions.

Skill Practice (20 minutes)

Description

Individuals or pairs—Each player practices dribbling. Players can choose the size and weight of the ball they use. At this point, you should provide players with situations in which they must dribble with either hand, without looking at the ball. Set up obstacles so players can learn to vary the force of the bounce. Here are some examples:

- Dribble in different pathways:
  — Play follow-the-leader with a partner (followers are three feet behind), changing to different pathways (see the bottom figure on page 66).
  — Design strategies to outwit an imaginary opponent from baseline to baseline.
- Dribble around stationary obstacles. Set up cone markers three feet apart. Players try to dribble for 60 seconds without bumping into the cones (see the top figure on page 67).
- Dribble around stationary players (see the bottom figure on page 67). Divide players into groups of 3 or 4. One player is the dribbler. The other players in the group become obstacles and arrange themselves in a zigzag obstacle pattern down the floor. The players try to cause the dribbler to lose control of the ball. They can stretch and pivot, but cannot move from their space; the defensive players cannot touch the ball or the dribbler. (You can make this activity more challenging by allowing the defensive players to touch the ball but not the dribbler, when the player is ready.)
- Dribble against an opponent. Match partners with similar skill levels. Partner 1 dribbles toward the baseline while partner 2 plays cooperative defense. Increase the difficulty by moving to active defense. If partner 2 takes the ball away before 30 seconds are up, he or she gives it back; after 30 seconds, partners switch roles.

Game 2 (10 minutes)

Goal

Players keep possession in order to score.

Description

Same as Game 1, except choose either 2 v 1 or 2 v 2, depending on the skill proficiency of your players. Rotate players accordingly so they all have a chance to play offense and defense.

Practice 5 (cont'd)

COACH's cues

"Keep your body between the obstacle and the ball."

"Keep the ball at your side."

Team Circle (5 minutes)

Key Idea: Responsibility

Gather children into a group near two cones about 10 feet apart. Choose two players to help role play. Set up a triangle of you and the two players. Let the children know you're role-playing with them. Each of you take turns passing. When it's your turn, miss the pass and role-play yourself as a player: "I couldn't get that pass! It was your fault—you made a bad pass!" Now as coach: "I want you to think about players who make excuses and blame others for their mistakes. Stand at this cone if you think it's okay to make excuses when you make mistakes. Stand at this cone if you think you should try to learn and work harder to improve." Ask players about their choices. "Not making excuses is taking responsibility for yourself."

Wrap-Up

Make summary comments about practice. Remind players of the next practice day and time and give them a sneak preview of that practice—passing and receiving with a partner and supporting the teammate with the ball.

COACH's point

☞ Demonstrate skills in slow motion and at regular speed.

Variations

Remember you can either ask players if they want to change the parameters of the game (such as the size of the ball or the court) or change them yourself in order to accommodate their abilities.

Practice 6

Warm-Up (10 minutes)

Individual—Players dribble from one basket to the next, and then jump stop and shoot. All shooting should be close to the basket (jump shots within two feet of the basket).

Fitness Circle (5 minutes)

Key Idea: Flexibility

Gather children in a group. Show them a rubber band or have them visualize one. Demonstrate how it stretches. "We pretend this rubber band is…" Wait for response—a muscle. "It moves back and forth, stretching and moving. Let's move our bodies just like the rubber band. Reach and stretch up and down. It's important to stretch slowly without bouncing or quick movement." Have children continue for one minute. "Our muscles help us to move and stretch. We need to stretch muscles to keep them flexible or able to move easily. When muscles can move easily they don't get injured and our bodies feel good."

Game 1 (10 minutes)

Goal

Players will pass and receive the ball and will support the teammate with the ball.

Description

3 v 2, modified half-court game—Three players play offense and two players defend, then two offensive players must switch roles with the defensive players. Switch at least twice so all players get to play defense. The team must pass three times before shooting. Limit them to

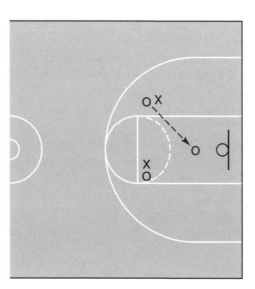

PURPOSE

To play a 3 v 2 game, focusing on keeping possession of the ball. The objective is for players to be able to pass and receive with a partner in order to score and to support teammates with the ball.

Equipment

- ☑ One basketball per player (if possible)
- ☑ One basketball short court, including two baskets per four players
- ☑ Tape or cones as markers (optional)
- ☑ Rubber band (optional)

97

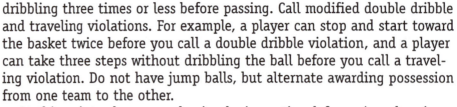

Practice 6 (cont'd)

dribbling three times or less before passing. Call modified double dribble and traveling violations. For example, a player can stop and start toward the basket twice before you call a double dribble violation, and a player can take three steps without dribbling the ball before you call a traveling violation. Do not have jump balls, but alternate awarding possession from one team to the other.

At this point, players can begin playing active defense (see description at beginning of chapter).

☞ The key in this practice is to get the players to move to an open space.

Coach: What is the goal of the game?
Players: The goal is to play as a team, passing and scoring.

Coach: How do you help each other out?
Players: We help by getting ready to receive a pass and moving around.

Skill Practice (20 minutes)

1. Introduce, demonstrate, and explain how to keep possession of the ball while moving it (see pages 119–122).
2. Have your players practice keeping possession of the ball while moving it.

Description

2 v 2—Two players dribble and pass while the other two players try to gain possession of the ball, either by intercepting a pass or stealing the ball on the dribble.

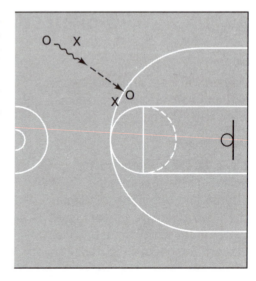

Practice 6

COACH's cues

"Keep your body between the ball and your opponent when dribbling."

"Change directions, speed, and pathways."

Game 2 (10 minutes)

Goal

Players will pass and receive and will support the teammate with the ball.

Description:

Same as Game 1.

Team Circle (5 minutes)

Key Idea: Caring

Gather children into a circle. Stand in the middle of the circle with a ball. Choose two children to pass the ball with you. "We're going to work on our passing skills." Pass repeatedly to them and not the others. "Tell me how you felt to have only two players get the passes." Listen to their responses. "Sharing the ball with your teammates shows you care about them. What other things can you do to show you care about your teammates?" Their responses should include encouragement, positive comments for good play, forgiving players who make mistakes, and so on. "Good. Those are all ways you can show you care."

Wrap-Up

Make summary comments about practice. Remind players of the next practice day and time and give them a sneak preview of that practice—defending against an opponent.

Practice 7

▶ PURPOSE

To defend your own space, focusing on basic defensive technique. The objective is for players to be able to defend an opponent.

Equipment

- ☑ One basketball per player (if possible)
- ☑ One basketball short court, including two baskets per four players
- ☑ Tape or cones as markers (optional)

Warm-Up (10 minutes)

Individual—Players dribble from one basket to the next, and then jump stop and shoot. All shooting should be close to the basket (jump shots within two feet of the basket).

Fitness Circle (5 minutes)

Key Idea: Muscular strength and endurance

Gather children into a group. "Okay, everyone get down on the ground and do the crab walk." Continue for 30 seconds to one minute. "Are your arms and legs getting tired? You used many of your arm and leg muscles to do the crab walk. What parts of the body do you use the most for basketball? That's right—your arms and legs. The more you practice basketball, the stronger your muscles will get. Then you can keep going much longer before you get too tired. What things can we do to get our muscles stronger for basketball?" Let them answer running and dribbling. "Right. Now pretend you have a basketball in front of you. Pretend to dribble the ball in your spot." Have children dribble for five counts. "Practicing dribbling helps make your arms stronger."

Game 1 (10 minutes)

Goal

Players will learn to use the basic defensive techniques.

Description

3 v 3, short-court game using modified half-court rules (see the figure on page 69)—The offensive team must pass three times before shooting. Limit them to dribbling three times or less before passing. Defensive players earn a point when they take the ball away without committing a foul. Call modified traveling violations. For example, a player can take three steps without dribbling the ball before you call a traveling violation. Do not have jump balls, but alternate awarding possession from one team to the other. Treat fouls like violations. Players should raise their hands when they foul.

Practice 1

Coach: What do you do when you are playing defense?
Players: Try to get the ball and protect the basket.

Coach: How do you defend your basket?
Players: Play the person with the ball and try to get the ball.

Skill Practice (20 minutes)

1. Introduce, demonstrate, and explain how to defend against an opponent (see pages 126–129).
2. Have your players practice defending against an opponent.

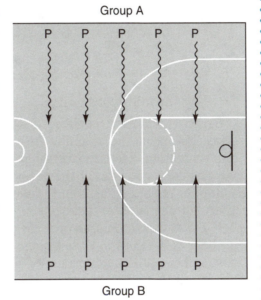

Description

All players—Divide players into two groups. The groups stand on opposite sidelines of the gym and face each other. Each member of group A has a ball to dribble. On a signal, group A begins dribbling toward the opposite sideline. Group B, without balls, begins moving forward, trying to take away the balls. If a group B player gains possession of a ball, that player dribbles toward the opposite sideline. When players from group A or group B make it over the opposing team's sideline, they stay there until all balls are behind the sidelines. Group B now gets the balls, and the game begins again.

"Keep your knees bent."
"Keep your body low."
"Put one hand up, one hand down."
"Keep a wide stance."

☞ Try not to get caught up in the details of defense. More will come later, when they are more developmentally ready. As we know, defense is hard work!

☞ If something is not working, change it! Use the KIS principle (Keep it successful).

Practice 1 (cont'd)

Game 2 (10 minutes)

Goal

Players use the basic defensive techniques.

Description

Same as Game 1, except choose either 1 v 3, 2 v 3, or 3 v 3, depending on the skill proficiency of your players. Rotate players accordingly so they all have a chance to play offense and defense.

Team Circle (5 minutes)

Key Idea: Responsibility

Gather children into a circle. "I want everyone to run in a circle, following the person in front of you, without bumping into each other. Keep a space about as long as a bicycle between you, and don't go ahead of the person in front of you." Encourage children to run slowly enough to follow all the directions. Continue activity for one minute. "Everyone stop. Did you bump into each other? Did anyone get upset with the person in front of you? You kept your body under control by not going ahead of the person in front of you. You kept your emotions under control by not getting upset with the person ahead of you—they couldn't move any faster since you were all running in a circle as a group. Everyone can stay safe and learn when everyone is responsible for themselves."

Wrap-Up

Make summary comments about practice. Remind players of the next practice day and time and give them a sneak preview of that practice—pressuring the ball handler.

Practice 8

Warm-Up (10 minutes)

Pairs—Partners take turns. One passes the ball, and the other either shoots from the Around the Key spots or dribbles and drives to the basket.

PURPOSE

To defend your own space, focusing on pressuring the ball handler. The objective is for players to be able to successfully steal the ball from an opponent.

Equipment

- ✓ One basketball per player (if possible)
- ✓ One basketball short court, including two baskets per four players
- ✓ Tape or cones as markers (optional)

Fitness Circle (5 minutes)

Key Idea: General fitness

Gather children into a circle. "What do our bodies need to do every day to keep going?" Wait for their responses. Discuss sleep and rest, eating, and doing regular activities. "There's one more thing that's really important—being active and exercising. Let's pretend it's a day that you do not have basketball practice. Your body needs to move every day. With no basketball today, what should we do to move our bodies?" Wait for their responses. If a child suggests an activity such as biking or swimming, have everyone act out that activity. Act out three activities. "It's important to be active when you don't have basketball practice. Your body needs to move every day."

Practice 8 (cont'd)

Game 1 (10 minutes)

Goal

Players will pressure the ball handler.

Description

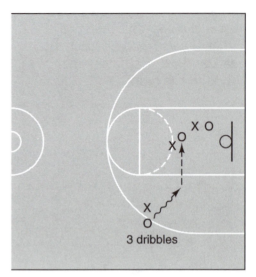

3 v 3, regular half-court game—Defensive players earn a point when they take the ball away without committing a foul. The offensive team must pass three times before shooting. Limit them to dribbling three times or less before passing. Call modified traveling violations. For example, a player can take three steps without dribbling the ball before you call a traveling violation. Do not have jump balls, but alternate awarding possession from one team to the other. Treat fouls like violations (players should raise their hands when they foul).

Follow regular half-court rules:

- If a team scores, the other team gets the ball at the top of the key (restart area).
- If a team gets an offensive rebound, that team can shoot again.
- If a team gets a defensive rebound, that team gets the ball at the top of the key (restart area).

Coach: What do you do when you try to steal the ball from an opponent?
Players: You watch the player, watch the ball, and try to figure out what the player will do.

Coach: How do you do that?
Players: You get low and keep your hands and feet active.

Practice 8

Skill Practice (20 minutes)

1. Introduce, demonstrate, and explain how to pressure the ball handler (see pages 126-127).
2. Have your players practice pressuring the ball handler.

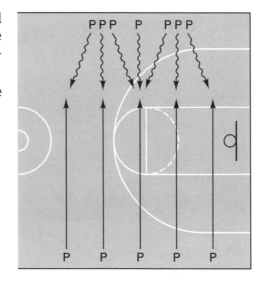

Description

All players—Divide players into two groups: a dribblers group, in which each player has a ball; and a defenders group, which does not have balls. The dribblers group should have more players. Keep the practice within a confined space. On a signal, the dribblers begin dribbling while the defenders attempt to steal the ball. If a defender steals a ball, he or she begins dribbling. Go for about 45 seconds, and then regroup and switch roles as needed.

COACH's cues

"Get into the ready position" (bend your knees; lower your body).
"Keep your hands and feet active."
"Watch the player; watch the ball."
"Anticipate."

Game 2 (10 minutes)

Goal
Players will pressure the ball handler.

Description
Same as Game 1, except choose either 1 v 3, 2 v 3, or 3 v 3, depending on the skill proficiency of your players. Rotate players accordingly so they all have a chance to play offense and defense.

Practice 8 (cont'd)

Team Circle (5 minutes)

Key Idea: Responsibility

Gather children into a circle. Stand in the center of the circle with a ball. Ask children to call to you and raise their hand if they are in a good position for a pass. Dribble the ball inside the circle, but do not pass to anyone. Continue for about one minute. "Did I share the ball with anyone?" Wait for their responses. "Do you think that is good teamwork? What *is* good teamwork?" Listen to their responses. Repeat the activity, but this time pass to players who call and raise their hands. "Teamwork is when all players are working together, not just keeping the ball to themselves. Responsible team members get in position to receive a good pass. They don't always pass to the same person. And they always work hard."

Wrap-Up

Make summary comments about practice. Remind players of the next practice day and time and give them a sneak preview of that practice—receiving a pass and shooting.

☞ Insist on no-contact, no-foul games. You may have to model for players how to maintain self-space in basketball, especially when a player has the ball (see the principle of verticality in chapter 9).

Practice 9

Warm-Up (10 minutes)

All players—Divide players into two groups: a dribblers group, in which each player has a ball, and a defenders group, which does not have balls (see the figure on page 105). The dribblers group should have more players. Keep the practice within a confined space. On a signal, the dribblers begin dribbling while the defenders attempt to steal the ball. If a defender steals a ball, he or she begins dribbling. Go for about 45 seconds, and then regroup and switch roles as needed.

Fitness Circle (5 minutes)

Key Idea: General fitness

Gather children into a circle. "Everyone is going to run in place. Let's start. Pretend that your body is going to run out of energy because you ate too many chips and drank a soda before practice. Start running slower and slower, and now stop! Now let's pretend that you ate a peanut butter sandwich and drank a glass of milk and a glass of water before practice. Let's run in place." Continue for 30 seconds. "See how you're able to run much longer and keep your energy? Eating healthy foods and drinking plenty of water are healthy habits for every day. You should drink water several times a day and drink even more when you're exercising. Also make sure to get enough sleep; exercise; brush your teeth; and say no to alcohol, tobacco, and other drugs. Keep your body healthy!"

Game 1 (10 minutes)

Goal

Players will score as often as possible.

Description

3 v 3, short-court game (use regular half-court rules)—Encourage players to score as much as possible. No dribbling is allowed in this game. Defensive players earn a point when they take the ball away

---

PURPOSE

To attack the basket, focusing on shooting within five to eight feet of the basket. The objective is for players to be able to receive a pass, square to the basket, and shoot accurately.

Equipment

- ✓ One basketball per two players (if possible)
- ✓ Half-court and one basket per four players
- ✓ Different colored vests or shirts (to differentiate teams)
- ✓ Tape or cones as markers (optional)

Practice 9 (cont'd)

without committing a foul. The offensive team must pass twice or more before shooting. Do not have jump balls, but alternate awarding possession from one team to the other. Treat fouls like violations.

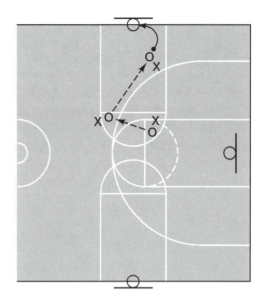

Coach: What is the goal of the game?
Players: The goal is to score following two consecutive passes.

Coach: From where on the court do you score most of your points?
Players: Most of the points are scored close to the basket.

Coach: Why is it better to shoot from a position close to the basket rather than far from the basket?
Players: You're more likely to score when you're closer (it's a high-percentage shot).

Coach: Besides shooting from close range, what else do you do to shoot successfully?
Players: We square our shoulders to the basket, keep our elbows under the ball and close to the body, keep one hand behind the ball and the other at the side of the ball, use a staggered stance with knees slightly bent, aim, and follow through.

Skill Practice (15 minutes)

1. Introduce, demonstrate, and explain how to receive a pass and shoot (see pages 121–125).
2. Have your players practice receiving a pass and shooting.

Description

Pairs—Partners take turns shooting three shots from each of five spots approximately five to eight feet away from the basket (see the figure on page 56). The partner not shooting rebounds the ball and passes it accurately to the shooting partner. The shooting partner gets in target position, receives the ball in triple threat position (see page 118), and squares up and shoots. Have players either count the number of baskets made or "high five" partners when they score a basket.

Practice 9

COACH's cues

for shooting
"Keep your hands apart on the ball."
"Only fingers touch the ball."
"Keep palms up."
"Point your elbows toward the basket."
"Flip your wrist and wave good-bye."

for triple threat
"Keep the ball on your hip."
"Keep your elbows out."
"Hold the ball to the side on your hip."

Game 2 (15 minutes)

Goal

Players will score as often as possible.

Description

Same as Game 1 except choose either 3 v 1, 3 v 2, or 3 v 3, depending on the skill proficiency of your players. Rotate players accordingly so they all have a chance to play offense and defense.

Team Circle (5 minutes)

Key Idea: Caring

Gather children into a group near the basket. Have a ball ready. Ask a child in the group to pass to you. Shoot at the basket and miss completely. Retrieve the ball and make a bad pass. "That shot wasn't very good, was it? How about that pass? Those were mistakes. What should you say to your teammates when they make mistakes?" Listen to their responses. "What could you say to make your teammate feel better? What could you could say to make her feel worse?" Listen to their responses. Have players change the unsupportive, negative comments to positive ones. "It's very important to forgive mistakes and be understanding of others, just as you would want them to be of you. Making mistakes is part of learning. Saying something that makes your teammates feel better shows you care about them."

Wrap-Up

Make summary comments about practice. Remind players of the next practice day and time and give them a sneak preview of that practice—supporting the ball handler.

COACH's point

☞ The goal is for players to have fun, balancing challenge and interest with frustration or boredom.

Practice 10

☞ PURPOSE

To play a 3 v 3 game, focusing on maintaining possession of the ball. The objective is for players to be able to pass quickly and accurately and to support the ball handler.

Equipment

- ☑ One basketball per player (if possible)
- ☑ One basketball short court, including two baskets per four players
- ☑ Tape or cones as markers (optional)

Warm-Up (10 minutes)

Pairs—Partners take turns shooting three shots from each of five spots marked around the basket (approximately six to eight feet away). The partner not shooting rebounds the ball and passes it accurately to the shooting partner. The shooting partner gets in target position, receives the ball in triple threat, and squares up and shoots (see the figure on page 56).

Fitness Circle (5 minutes)

Key Idea: General fitness

Gather children into a group near two cones about 10 feet apart. Tell them that each cone represents a different food group. "This cone is healthy foods, such as fruits, vegetables, meats, milk, and breads. This other cone is special treat foods, such as chips, soda, candy, and sweet snacks. What foods can you eat to keep your body healthy, with enough energy for basketball?" As they respond, have them stand near the cone they choose. "It is important to eat more healthy foods. They give you more energy for basketball and help you grow. Special treat foods should be eaten in small amounts. Can you tell me other examples of healthy foods and special treat foods?"

Game 1 (10 minutes)

Goal

Players will support the ball handler.

Description

3 v 3, short-court game using regular half-court rules (see the figure on page 69)—The team must pass three times before shooting. Limit them to dribbling three times or less before passing. Call modified traveling violations. For example, a player can take three steps without dribbling the ball before you call a traveling violation. Do not have jump balls, but alternate awarding possession from one team to the other. Treat fouls like violations. A field goal is worth two points.

Practice 10

Coach: What is the goal of the game?
Players: The goal is to shoot as often as possible, to pass and shoot.

Coach: What do you do to help your teammate with the ball?
Players: We move to get open.

Skill Practice (15 minutes)

Description

2 v 1, in an area the size of the basketball lane—Two offensive players, an attacker (O) and a supporter (S), play against one defensive player (X). On the whistle, the defender attacks the ball (cooperative to active defense), the supporter moves to either side, and the attacker draws the defender and then passes. The practice continues until either the offensive players have made three passes or the defender has possession of the ball.

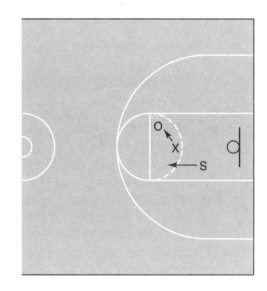

COACH's cues

"Move quickly to the side." (Cue for the supporter)

"Attack the ball." (Cue for the defender)

"Pass as the defender advances." (Cue for the attacker)

COACH's point

☞ Try to get players to make razor-edge cuts with quick bursts of energy. Be sure to model the practice activities and model the cut.

Practice 10 (cont'd)

Game 2 (15 minutes)

Goal

Players will support the ball handler.

Description

Same as Game 1, except choose either 3 v 1, 3 v 2, or 3 v 3, depending on the skill proficiency of your players. Rotate players accordingly so they all have a chance to play offense and defense.

Team Circle (5 minutes)

Key Idea: Respect

Gather children into a group. "What have you learned about basketball this season?" Listen to their responses. "What does respect have to do with playing basketball or any sports? It takes many years to master the game of basketball, so basketball deserves your respect. Every year there are new skills to learn and improve on; every year you play, you'll get better. That's why you need to come back next year! What examples of players showing respect have you seen this basketball season?" Listen to their responses and discuss.

Wrap-Up

Make summary comments about what players learned over the season. Encourage players to come back next year!

Variations

If needed, return to a 2 v 2 or 3 v 2 game.

Part III

The Building Blocks

In part II, we provided you with the plans for coaching basketball, starting with the season plans for teaching four- through seven-year-olds the basics of basketball and other important fitness and character development concepts, and then going into detailed plans for conducting each practice session. In part III, we'll assist you by presenting more information about how to teach the subject matter planned in part II.

In chapter 8, we'll review how to teach basic basketball skills, and in chapter 9, we'll examine the rules of the game and a few unwritten traditions that are useful to know. In chapter 10, we'll tell you more about the basic fitness and safety concepts we want you to integrate into your teaching of basketball, and in chapter 11, we'll do the same for character development concepts.

The better you understand the subject matter of what you teach, the better you're likely to teach it. The information in this book is a good starting point, but feel free to learn more by exploring some of the resources listed in appendix A at the end of this book.

chapter 8

Teaching Basketball Skills and Tactics

This is where we'll give you more in-depth in-formation about the skills and tactics you'll be teaching to your YMCA Rookies players. Some of the skills described in this chapter are not included in the practice plans, but they are included here for coaches who have advanced players ready for a higher level of play. The skills that we'll describe for you include individual skills of position and movement, ballhandling, and defense. Each skill will be illustrated and will include suggestions for how to correct common errors in execution.

This chapter covers the basic basketball skills you'll want your players to learn. Remember to start with the most basic skills and slowly advance players through more difficult techniques. Monitor players' understanding of each new skill by asking them specific questions about the skill and watching them attempt to perform it. Then you won't lose them along the way as you advance your skill instruction.

 ## Position and Movement

Many coaches take for granted their players' ability to position and move around the court. Don't! You'll save a lot of time and increase your players' effectiveness if you emphasize proper footwork in every one of your practices. This footwork includes the jump stop; pivots, cuts, slides; and the triple threat position.

The Jump Stop

One of the most common violations that beginners commit is traveling, usually due to poor stopping skills. You'll want to help your players learn how to start and stop with their bodies under control. Young players need to learn the jump stop so they can stop after moving quickly either with or without the ball.

To practice the jump stop, have players begin in the ready position. In the ready position, players stand relaxed with arms and legs bent, feet shoulder-width apart, and weight shifted slightly forward to the balls of the feet (see figure 8.1). Blow your whistle and have your players sprint forward five or six steps. When they hear your whistle the second time, have them stop quickly with both feet simultaneously hitting the floor, landing in a balanced and ready position.

By using the jump stop, players are able to gather and control their forward momentum and may use either foot as a pivot foot for offensive moves. Practice this simple stop often. Until beginning players learn how to control their momentum, either with or without the ball, they will be playing out of control.

Pivots, Cuts, and Slides

After players have mastered the jump stop, you'll want to help them with some other basic footwork:

Figure 8.1   Ready position.

◎ Turning or pivoting on either foot to change direction.

◎ Pushing off either foot when running to cut quickly.

◎ Sliding their feet on defense without crossing them.

Pivots

Along with mastering the jump stop, learning to pivot correctly will give players a lot of confidence in their footwork. A pivot simply involves stopping and then turning on one foot to move forward (front pivot) or dropping one foot backward (back pivot), all while keeping the ball of one foot on the court (see figure 8.2).

Remind players that after using a jump stop they may choose either foot as their pivot foot, but they may not change that pivot foot while in possession of the ball. Each time they receive the ball, they should assume the ready position, and then they may use their pivot foot to do one of the following:

◎ Pivot to protect the ball from the defense.

◎ Pivot to pass to a teammate.

◎ Pivot to make a move to the basket.

Teaching Basketball Skills and Tactics

Cuts

The ability to change direction quickly and in balance (to cut) is important on both the offensive and the defensive ends of the court. Offensive players will have trouble getting open for passes or shots if they cannot lose their opponents with quick cuts. Defenders will have a hard time keeping up with effective offensive players if they are unable to respond to various cuts.

Teach your players how to cut on the court by having them practice planting one foot on the court at the end of a stride, and then pushing off that foot to shift their momentum in another direction. For example, tell players to push off with the left foot if they wish to cut to the right. They should then turn the unplanted foot in the direction they want to go and lead with that leg as they burst toward the new direction. When cutting, players should bend their knees to lower their center of gravity and provide explosiveness to their legs.

Figure 8.2 Pivot.

Effective cuts are hard, sharp, and explosive. Three very effective cuts used by offensive players to get open are the L-cut, V-cut, and backdoor cut (see figure 8.3).

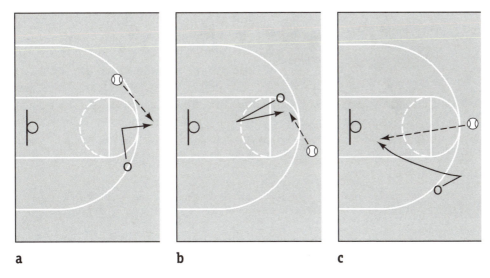

Figure 8.3 *(a)* L-cut, *(b)* V-cut, *(c)* backdoor cut.

117

ERROR DETECTION AND CORRECTION FOR PIVOTING

Error

Moving and switching the pivot foot while in possession of the ball

Correction

1. Teach players to use the jump stop so they can pivot on either foot (see figure 8.4).

2. Teach players to pivot away from the defensive pressure and square up to face the basket as soon as they receive the ball.

3. Remind players that once they choose a pivot foot, they cannot lift that foot from or slide it across the floor.

4. Encourage players to take full advantage of their ability to pivot in either direction as long as they keep the ball of the pivot foot in the same spot.

Figure 8.4 The jump stop allows players to pivot on either foot.

Slides

Basketball defenders must be able to slide their feet and maintain an arm's distance from their opponent, who is attempting to drive or cut to the basket. But youngsters are much more comfortable with forward than with lateral movement and thus tend to cross their feet when attempting to move sideways. Therefore, you will need to take time to teach and drill them to slide their feet effectively.

Instruct players to stand in the ready position and then move the leg nearest their intended direction about two feet to that side. Next, they should slide the other foot until the feet once again are shoulder-width apart (see figure 8.5). Remind players to keep their toes pointed forward and to move as quickly as possible on the balls of their feet. They'll be able to slide more quickly if they keep their knees bent, rears down, and backs erect.

Triple Threat Position

The triple threat position is a version of the ready position in which the player holds the ball to the side on the hip, with elbows out (see figure 8.6). This position gives the player the options of either shooting, passing, or dribbling. Such a position makes the defender uncertain of what the ballhandler will do, and it gives the ballhandler a number of choices.

a  b

Figure 8.5 Lateral slide.

 ## Ballhandling Skills

A key to success in basketball is moving the ball effectively into a position where a player can take shots that have a good chance of being successful. The skills of passing, receiving, dribbling, and shooting are therefore essential to success in basketball.

Passing

Passing is an offensive skill used to maintain possession and create scoring opportunities. Passes should usually be short and crisp, because long or slow passes are likely to be stolen by an opposing player. Players should avoid throwing too hard or using passes that are difficult to control, however. Players should pass the ball above the waist and within easy reach of the receiver. If possible, passes should be thrown to the receiver's side that is farthest from her or his defender. As your players become more skilled, work with them on faking a pass one way and then passing another way.

Keep it simple at the beginning by starting your players with these two types of passes:

- Chest pass
- Bounce pass

Figure 8.6 Triple threat position.

Chest Pass

An often overlooked element of good passing is how to use the legs to generate the momentum for a pass. Begin by teaching your players to start in ready position and to always step toward their target to initiate the pass. The chest pass, shown in figure 8.7, is so named because the passer uses two hands to throw the ball from his or her chest to the receiver's chest area. Teach your players to throw the pass so that their thumbs snap down and together.

Bounce Pass

Sometimes it is easier for a passer to get the ball to a teammate by bouncing the ball once on the court before it reaches the receiver. For example, a defender may be guarding a player with both hands overhead, preventing a pass through the air to a teammate. In that case, a bounce pass may be the only route to get the ball to a teammate. Instruct your players to use bounce passes when they are closely guarded and don't have the space to extend their arms in a chest pass.

Figure 8.7   Chest pass.

Teach players to bounce the ball on the court two-thirds of the way between themselves and the receiver, as illustrated in figure 8.8. Remind them to use their legs and to step toward the target. Snapping their thumbs down and together as they release the pass will give the ball some backspin. Backspin will slow the pass down a little as it hits the floor and give the receiver a chance to catch the ball at waist level in the ready position.

Figure 8.8   Bounce pass.

Receiving

Even the best passes are of little value if they aren't caught. Sloppy receiving technique is often the cause of turnovers and missed scoring opportunities. Emphasize the following receiving techniques:

- Show a target to the passer (put an arm up or out to the side) and call for the ball.
- Move to meet the pass; step toward the ball, not away.
- Watch the ball come into your hands.
- Use two hands to catch the ball; the palms should face the passer, and thumbs should be together.

In most situations after receiving a pass, players should come to a jump stop, with their feet positioned shoulder-width apart in ready position. From this position, players should pivot to face the basket and look for an open teammate, a shot, or a lane to dribble the ball to the basket.

Dribbling

If there's one thing that young players like to do when they get their hands on a basketball, it's to bounce it. Unfortunately, when they practice on their own, only a few players dribble correctly. Therefore, you'll need to teach your players how to dribble effectively and watch that they use the correct dribbling technique, as shown in figure 8.9.

Teaching players correct dribbling technique is difficult because most of them have already established incorrect dribbling habits. The three most common errors of self-taught young dribblers are slapping at the ball from the chest area and waiting for it to bounce back up; keeping the head down, with eyes riveted to each bounce; and using one hand exclusively to bounce the ball.

As you correct these dribbling errors and attempt to improve your players' dribbling skills, give the players this advice:

- Establish a feel for the ball with the fingerpads.
- Maintain the ready position, keeping knees bent and rear down.
- Keep the dribble under control, and always bounce the ball below waist height, even lower when you're being guarded closely.
- Bounce the ball close to the body and protect the dribble from the defender with the non-dribbling hand and arm.
- Keep your head up and see the rest of the court (and teammates!).
- Learn how to dribble with the right and left hands.
- Keep practicing!

Figure 8.9 Correct dribbling technique.

Dribbling Dos and Don'ts

Dos

- Keep the dribble alive until you have a shot or an open teammate to pass to.
- Vary the speed and direction of the dribble so defenders are kept off guard.
- Protect the dribble from the defensive player with the non-dribbling arm when being closely guarded.
- Switch dribbling hands to protect the ball after dribbling past a defender.
- Stay in the middle of the court and away from the sidelines and corners to avoid being trapped.

Don'ts

- Automatically start dribbling after receiving a pass. Look to see what shooting or passing options are available after squaring up to the basket.
- Pick up the ball or stop dribbling with no other option (shot or pass) available.
- Dribble into a crowd—the ball is more likely to be stolen.
- Try to get fancy when good fundamental dribbling will do the job.
- Hesitate. Be assertive and confident when dribbling the ball.

Shooting

Every player loves to put the basketball through the hoop. Your players will be highly motivated to learn proper shooting technique if you convince them that it will help them make more of their shots.

To get the fundamentals of shooting across and encourage your players to learn them, tell them they'll SCORE if they do these things:

S Select only high-percentage shots (shots that are likely to go in).

C Concentrate on their target.

O Order movements: square up, bend knees and elbows, and cock wrist.

R Release and wave good-bye to the ball (have the shooting hand follow through).

E Extend the shooting arm up and out toward the basket.

Players can shoot the ball in a variety of ways, including set shots, jump shots, and layups.

Teaching Basketball Skills and Tactics

Set and Jump Shots

Although the most common shot at higher levels of play is the jump shot, young players who lack the leg strength and coordination to spring from the floor while shooting will more often shoot set shots. So teach your players the mechanics of the set shot first, and they will be able to advance to the jump shot as they increase strength and improve coordination.

Teach your players these shooting mechanics in this sequence:

1. Lay the ball on the fingerpads of each hand, with the shooting hand behind and slightly underneath the ball and the non-shooting hand balancing the ball from the side.

2. Focus on a specific target, usually the rim or backboard. The middle of the rim should be the target for most shots, but when you're at a 30- to 60-degree angle from the hoop, you should target the corner of the square on the backboard for a bank shot (see figure 8.10a).

3. Align shoulders, hips, and feet square with (facing) the basket. The foot on the shooting hand side can be up to six inches in front of the other foot so that the base of support is comfortable and balanced.

4. Bend the knees to get momentum for the shot. Let the legs, not the arms, be the primary power source for the shot.

5. Bend the shooting arm's elbow to approximately a 90-degree angle, keeping the forearm perpendicular to the floor and in front of the cocked wrist, as you raise the ball to the shooting position above the forehead (see figure 8.10b).

6. As you extend the legs, release the ball by extending the elbow, bringing the wrist forward and moving the fingers of the shooting hand up and

a

Figure 8.10 Proper technique for a jump shot.

(continued)

123

Coaching YMCA Rookies Basketball

through the ball (see figure 8.10c). The non-shooting arm and hand should maintain their supportive position on the side of the ball until after the release.

7. Follow through after the release by landing on both feet, extending the shooting arm and dropping the wrist, pointing the index finger of the shooting hand directly at the basket.

For several practices, your players will probably have difficulty shooting the ball properly. The reason is that they've developed bad shooting habits and the correct shooting motion is awkward for them. Check that your players aren't shooting "line drives" at the hoop. Help them to see how important proper arc is in allowing the shot a reasonable chance to go in. Remind them to shoot the ball up, then out, toward the basket.

b

c

Figure 8.10 *(continued)*

Teaching Basketball Skills and Tactics

ERROR DETECTION AND CORRECTION FOR SHOOTING

Error

Dribbling before shooting when open, and within good shooting range, or without a clear path to the basket

Correction

1. Receive the pass and pivot to face the basket in the ready position.

2. Hold the ball in preparation for a shot or a two-handed pass.

3. Check where the defense is positioned, whether a shot is open, and whether a teammate closer to the basket is open (see figure 8.11).

4. If the nearest defender does not deny the shot and no teammate is open for a higher percentage shot, shoot the ball.

Layups

The highest percentage shot, and therefore the most desirable shot, is a layup. A layup is a one-handed shot taken within three feet of the basket (see figure 8.12 on page 126). While we don't teach layups in the Rookies practice plans, you may have advanced players who are ready to attempt them.

Teach players to use their left hands when shooting layups from the left side of the basket and their right hands when shooting from the right side of the basket. The layup motion begins with the player planting and exploding (much like a high jumper) off the foot opposite the shooting hand, after striding from a 45-degree angle to the hoop. The player explodes off the planted foot straight up into the air. At the top of the jump, the player releases the ball by bringing the shooting hand, which is underneath the ball and near the shoulder, up toward the basket.

As in the set shot, the index finger of the shooting hand should be pointed directly at the basket or the appropriate spot on the backboard. Teach beginning players always to use the backboard on their layups. It gives them a steady target to aim for every time.

Your right-handed players are likely to find left-handed layups troublesome, just as your left-handed players are going to find right-handed layups

Figure 8.11 Check for defensive positioning.

125

difficult. Point out to them the reason for using the hand farthest from the basket to shoot the ball: the ball is more easily protected.

Then walk them through the proper footwork: they take one step with their left foot and explode up to shoot with no dribble on the right side. Then have them back up and step with their right foot, then step with the left foot, and shoot. Finally, have them back up and dribble once, stepping right, then stepping left, and shooting. Repeat this walk-through (no dribble) on the left side. Once they get the mechanics down without worrying about dribbling, they can speed up their approach and add the drive.

 Defensive Skills

The individual defensive skills of basketball are sometimes less appreciated than the individual offensive techniques, but they are just as important. Kids need to learn the basics of player-to-player defense from the outset if they are to compete successfully in skill practices and games. The skills described here include moving the feet, guarding an opponent with the ball, guarding an opponent away from the ball, and rebounding.

Moving the Feet

From the ready position, a defender can move quickly in any direction and maintain balance. Have your players practice sliding in short, quick, lateral bursts (as described on page 118) from one point to another, without crossing their feet.

Figure 8.12 Proper technique for a layup.

Emphasize to your players to keep their feet active on defense and not to reach and get off balance. Even the best defensive players can get beat momentarily, however. Tell your players that, when an offensive player gains an advantage by moving past them, they should turn and sprint to catch up and reestablish position.

Guarding an Opponent With the Ball

Obviously, the reason for guarding offensive players with the ball is to prevent them from scoring. A defender can best accomplish this goal by staying between his or her assigned opponent and the basket. Maintaining an arm's distance from the offensive player with the ball is a good rule of thumb.

Tell your players to consider these questions concerning their bodies and court positions when guarding a player with the ball:

◉ Body position
  —Am I in ready position and alert?
  —Am I an arm and a half's distance from my player with the ball and able to put pressure on his or her ability to shoot, pass, or drive?

◉ Court position
  —Is my player close enough to attempt a good shot?
  —Am I close enough to the player to prevent an easy shot?
  —Am I too close, so the opponent can drive around me?
  —Will a teammate be able to help me if the player beats me with the dribble?

Have your players focus on their opponent's midsection. If defenders watch the ball or their opponent's head or feet, they are likely to react to a fake that will put them out of defensive position.

As the offensive player begins to dribble, the defender should react by sliding his or her feet and maintaining an arm's distance from the opponent, trying to beat the offensive player to the spot that the player wants to reach. If the defender can get the offensive player to stop and pick up the ball, the defender can then move closer and crowd the offensive player by blocking the passing lanes, applying extensive pressure with the arms.

Guarding an Opponent Away From the Ball

Defending an opponent without the ball is just as important as guarding a player with the ball, but it is a bit more complicated. Whether an opponent is just one pass away from the ball or as many as two passes away, defensive players need to learn the defensive concept of ball-player-self (see figure 8.13). Defenders want to position themselves so they can see the ball (and know whether they need to come and help a teammate on a pass or drive), and they must keep track of a moving opponent (their player) who may be trying to get open to receive a pass.

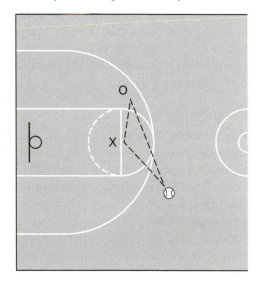

Figure 8.13 Ball-player-self concept.

Error Detection and Correction for Guarding Away From the Ball

Error

Defenders away from the ball losing track of where their offensive player is on the court

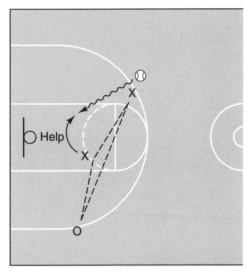

Figure 8.14 A player two or more passes away needs to stay alert.

Correction

1. Position players to see the ball and their player without turning their head (see "Open Position" below).
2. Have players establish and maintain the ball-player-self relationship.
3. Have players point at the ball with one hand and their player with the other.
4. Have players adjust positions as the offensive player or ball changes position.
5. A player two or more passes away needs to be alert to help out on a drive or deflect a long pass attempt to their opponent in the corner (see figure 8.14).

Denial Position

Teach your players to use the denial position when their opponent is one pass away from the ball. The space between two offensive players where a pass can be made is called the passing lane. A defender wants to have an arm and leg in the passing lane when guarding a player who is one pass away (see figure 8.15). This denial position allows the defender to establish the ball-player-self relationship and discourages the offensive player with the ball from even attempting a pass.

Open Position

When offensive players are two or more passes away from the ball, the defensive player wants to establish an open position that still maintains the ball-player-self relationship. In the open position, the defender is farther away from the offensive player, pointing to the ball with one hand and the opponent with the other hand (see figure 8.16). Using peripheral vision, the defender moves to react as the ball penetrates toward the basket (to help out on the drive) or into denial position if the offensive player cuts hard to receive a pass. In both the denial and open positions, the key is remembering always to maintain the ball-player-self relationship.

Figure 8.15 Denial position.

Figure 8.16 Open position.

Rebounding

Rebounding, or gaining possession of a missed shot is not a skill that is taught in the Rookies practice plans. However, it is a basic basketball skill that players will need to learn as they continue playing. When players rebound, they do not stand and watch the shot to see if it goes in. Instead, they learn to position themselves advantageously for rebounds (as shown in figure 8.17).

If you teach your players to rebound, you also must warn them to avoid reaching over an opponent for a rebound. They'll get called for a foul if they do. Emphasize the importance of jumping straight up for the rebound. Not only will a vertical jump achieve greater height, but players will avoid needless fouls if they go straight up.

Here are some additional rebounding tips:

- A shot taken from the side is very likely to rebound to the opposite side of the basket. Therefore, players should try to get position on the opposite side of the basket when such a shot is taken.
- Once contact is established with an opposing player, the defensive rebounder should maintain that contact until he or she jumps for the rebound.
- After controlling a rebound, players should keep the ball at chin level with their elbows out (see figure 8.18).

Figure 8.17 Boxing out on the rebound.

Figure 8.18 Proper rebounding position.

chapter 9

Teaching Basketball Rules and Traditions

This chapter is where we'll introduce you to some of the basic rules and traditions of basketball. We won't try to cover all the rules of the game, but we'll give you what you need to work with four- to seven-year-old children. Some of the rules will be explained just so you understand the game better; those that should be taught to your players have been incorporated into the practice plans.

In this chapter, we'll give you information on ball and court size and markings, player equipment, player positions, actions to start and restart the game, fouls and violations, and scoring. In a short section, we'll show you the officiating signals for basketball. We also will talk briefly about a few of the unwritten rules or traditions of basketball, which good players follow to be courteous and safe.

 ## Ball and Court Characteristics

Because basketball is a game in which a ball is passed, dribbled, and shot with the hands, the size of the ball must be appropriate for participants. A regulation men's basketball is far too heavy and large for kids to handle. For YMCA Rookies, we recommend you use a #5 ball, and, if possible, supply balls in a variety of sizes and weights.

Basketball courts are normally 50 feet by 94 feet (84 feet in high school), but this size is much too large for children younger than eight. YMCA Rookies should play on smaller-sized courts, either half-court or a short court (the basket is at the side of the court). We also recommend that you lower the basket from the regulation 10 feet to 6 feet for the six- to seven-year-olds and to 5 feet for the four- to five-year-olds.

Figure 9.1 shows the standard basketball court markings. Those you will use most often in YMCA Rookies play are the sidelines, the midcourt line, and the free-throw lane (or *key*). Several areas of the court are referred to with special basketball terminology:

◉ *Frontcourt* refers to the half of the court where your team's offensive basket is located.

◉ *Backcourt* includes the midcourt line and the half of the court where your opponent's basket is located.

◉ The *three-second lane* is an area that extends from the baseline under the basket to the free-throw line; it's also called the *key*. The semicircle that extends beyond the free-throw line designates the *top of the key*. In regulation play, offensive players are not allowed to remain in the lane for more than three seconds. If they do, a violation is called, and the ball is given to the opposing team. This violation will not be called in YMCA Rookies, however.

◉ The area outside the three-second lane area is called the *perimeter*.

◉ The *three-point line* marks a semicircle that is 19 feet from the basket at all points. Shots that are made from behind this line count for three points instead of two.

◉ The square markings six feet from the baseline on each side of the lane are referred to as the *blocks*.

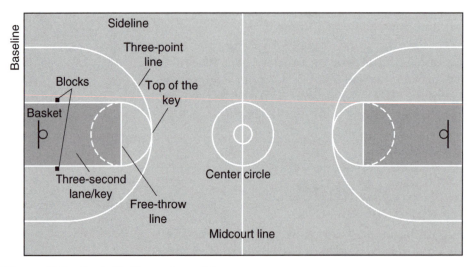

Figure 9.1 Basketball court markings.

Player Equipment

Basketball requires very little equipment. Players should wear basketball shoes so they have proper traction on the court, and we recommend that they wear two pairs of athletic socks to avoid blisters. They should wear clothing such as athletic shorts and tank tops or loose-fitting shirts so they have the freedom of movement needed to run, jump, and shoot. Players may choose to wear safety glasses or goggles to protect their eyes from injury. Also, if desired, players who have conditions affecting the knees or elbows may want to wear soft pads to protect them.

Player Positions

Although in YMCA Rookies your players will only play 2 v 2 or 3 v 3, basketball is usually played with five players on a team. Each player is assigned a position, and each position is referred to by a number (1 through 5). The types of positions are guard, forward, and center.

- **Guards.** Guards usually are the best ballhandlers and outside shooters on the team. They tend to be shorter and quicker than the other players and to have good dribbling and passing skills. Guards play farthest from the basket, on the perimeter.

   A basketball team usually has two guards in the game at all times. The point guard, who is in the #1 position, is played by the team's best dribbler and passer. The second guard is the off guard, who is in the #2 position. He or she is often the team's best long-range shooter and second-best dribbler.

- **Forwards.** Forwards typically are taller than guards and play near the basket. They should be able to shoot the ball accurately from within 12 feet of the basket and rebound the ball when shots are missed.

   A team usually plays with two forwards in its lineup. The small forward (also referred to as the *wing*) is in the #3 position. This position often is filled by the most versatile and athletic member of the team. The small forward must be able to play in the lane and on the perimeter on offense and to guard small and quick or big and strong opponents on defense. The other forward position is the big forward, the #4 position. This is a good spot to assign one of your bigger players and better rebounders who can also shoot the ball from anywhere in the lane area.

- **Center.** The center, or #5 position (also called the *post position*), is frequently the tallest or biggest player on the team. That extra size is helpful in maneuvering for shots or rebounds around the basket. A tall center can also make it difficult for opposing teams to shoot near the basket. A center should have soft hands to catch the passes thrown into the lane area by guards and forwards. Most basketball teams designate one player on the court as their center.

Starting and Restarting the Game

In regulation play, a jump ball at center court is used to start games and overtime periods, which are played when teams are tied at the end of regulation time. During jump balls, the official tosses up the ball between two players, usually each team's center or best leaper. Each player attempts to tip the ball to a teammate (who must be outside of the center circle) to gain possession of the ball. Another jump ball situation occurs after simultaneous possession of the ball by players from opposing teams. In this case, teams alternate possession; the team that did not win the first jump ball takes the ball out of bounds in the next jump ball situation.

In YMCA Rookies, jump balls are not used to begin a game. Teams decide who starts the game by tossing a coin, guessing a number, or following some other fair procedure. Play stops when the ball goes out of bounds and when the coach calls a violation or a foul.

 ## Fouls

Basketball can be a contact sport, with players often in close proximity and in constant motion. The rules of the game discourage rough play or tactics that allow a team to gain an advantage through brute force. Fouls are called when officials see illegal physical contact between two or more players based on these general principles:

- The first player to establish position (to become stationary or set) on the court has priority rights to that position.
- A body part cannot be extended into the path of an opponent.
- The player who moves into the path of an opponent, especially an airborne opponent, when contact occurs is responsible for the contact.
- All players have the right to the space extending straight up from their feet on the floor. This right is called the *principle of verticality*.

Types of Fouls

Based on the general principles concerning player contact, these specific fouls are called in a regulation game:

- *Blocking* is physically impeding the progress of another player who is still moving.
- *Charging* is running into or pushing a defender who is stationary.
- *Holding* is restricting the movement of an opponent.
- *Over-the-back* is infringing on the vertical plane of, and making contact with, a player who is in position and attempting to rebound.

- *Reaching in* is extending an arm and making contact with a ballhandler in an attempt to steal the ball.
- *Tripping* is extending a leg or foot and causing an opponent to lose balance or fall.

One other foul is an illegal screen, in which an offensive person tries to block a defender and makes contact. However, screens are not used in YMCA Rookies play.

The fouls just described are called *personal fouls*. This list covers most common ones, although there are others. Another type of possible foul is a *shooting foul*, in which a defender makes contact with a player who is shooting the basketball. (Other types of fouls exist, such as *intentional, technical,* and *flagrant,* but these relate to extreme behaviors by players and should not come up with YMCA Rookies players.) Emphasize to your players the importance of keeping hands off the shooter, establishing position, using the feet more than the arms to play defense, and not attempting to rebound over an opponent who has established position.

Consequences of Fouls

A team that fouls too much pays for it. Fouls carry with them increasingly severe penalties. A player who has five fouls is taken out of the game. In regulation play, a team that has more than a specified number of fouls in a quarter or half gives the opposing team a bonus situation: the member of the team who was fouled is allowed to shoot free throws (shoot from the free throw line with no opposition). If the foul is made on a player who is not shooting, that player shoots one free throw and, if he or she makes it, shoots a second one (this is called *one-and-one*). If the foul is made on a player who is shooting, that player shoots two free throws. Table 9.1 lists the types of fouls and their consequences.

TABLE 9.1

Fouls and Consequences

Type of foul	Team fouled in bonus?	Penalty
Shooting	Yes/No	Two free throws
Personal	No	Ball out of bounds
Personal	Yes	One-and-one free throws

Communicating After Fouls

How you discuss fouls with players is important. You want to discourage rough and dirty play, but you don't want to make players fearful of fouling. Hustling young players will inevitably pick up some fouls in each game. When a foul is called, point out to the player who fouled why the violation was called and explain to him or her how the foul could have been avoided with a more effective action. Although free throws are used in regulation play, they are not used in YMCA Rookies. Instead, treat fouls as violations, awarding the ball to the opposing team.

 Violations

Ballhandling violations occur more often than fouls in youth basketball. The *turnovers* (losses of the ball to the defense) caused by these violations will be one of your continuing frustrations as a basketball coach.

Types of Violations

These miscues are common among young ballhandlers:

- *Double dribble* is resuming dribbling after having stopped (when no defender interrupts the player's possession of the ball) or dribbling with both hands at the same time.
- *Charging*, which was described as a foul before, is also recorded as a turnover by the offense.
- *Over-and-back* is the return of the ball to the backcourt by an offensive player after he or she has crossed into the frontcourt.
- *Traveling* is taking more than one step without dribbling; it is also called *carrying the ball* or *palming the ball* when a player turns the ball a complete rotation in the hand between dribbles.

In YMCA Rookies play, double dribble and traveling rules are modified at first and gradually become closer to regulation rules. An over-and-back violation cannot happen in YMCA Rookies play, because games are not played on a full court. In regulation play, violations can be called for various time restrictions, such as how long it takes to get the ball across the midcourt line or how long offensive players can stand in the lane. These violations are not called in YMCA Rookies play.

Communicating After Violations

Basketball coaches generally distinguish between errors of commission and errors of omission when talking to their players. Errors of commission are mistakes associated with effort, such as a foul committed while hustling for a loose ball. Unless players are playing out of control, don't reprimand them after errors of commission. On the other hand, errors of omission, which are failures to perform assigned duties or within the rules, must be brought to players' attention. A player may simply be unaware of the role that was not fulfilled or the rule that was not followed. Whatever the case, calmly explain to him or her what is necessary to correct the performance.

Scoring

In regulation play, teams are awarded two points for every field goal. (When players are old enough to shoot successfully from behind the three-point line, they can earn three points.) A successful free throw is worth one point. The team that wins the most points over the course of the game is the winner.

In YMCA Rookies, you will find that we recommend that players be given some additional ways to score points, such as earning a point for keeping possession of the ball. This scoring system helps players focus on particular skills as they play.

Officiating Signals

Even though your YMCA Rookies basketball practices won't be officiated, you may want to use the officiating signals to indicate fouls or violations. If you use the correct signals, the players will get used to the signals and their meaning. Figures 9.2 a–t (on pages 138–140) show some common officiating signals.

Basketball Traditions

Young children only need to know a couple of unwritten laws for basketball, and both of those are based on the core values. First, players should raise their hands if they know they've fouled someone. This admission is especially important in YMCA Rookies games because an official won't be watching. Admitting when you've committed a foul is an example of being honest.

Second, players should play cooperatively with those on their team and should show respect for their opponents. This is showing respect for others. They should shake hands with their opponents after the game to thank them for playing hard and providing a good game. Players usually line up on the sideline next to the benches to shake hands with each other.

Figure 9.2 Officiating signals for *(a)* start clock, *(b)* stop clock for jump ball, *(c)* beckon substitute when ball is dead and clock is stopped, *(d)* stop clock for foul, *(e)* one point scored, *(f)* two points scored, *(g)* three points scored.

(continued)

Figure 9.2 *(continued)* Officiating signals for *(h)* blocking, *(i)* bonus situation (for second throw, drop one arm), *(j)* over-and-back or carrying the ball, *(k)* pushing, *(l)* illegal use of hands, *(m)* technical foul.

Figure 9.2 *(continued)* Officiating signals for *(n)* three-second violation, *(o)* designates out-of-bounds spot, *(p)* traveling, *(q)* holding, *(r)* no score, *(s)* hand checking, *(t)* illegal dribble.

chapter 10

Teaching Fitness and Safety

As a coach, you have a great opportunity to teach your players not only about basketball, but also about fitness and health. The attitudes and the knowledge they learn now can be a foundation for their future fitness. And you don't have to be a fitness expert to do this. We've supplied you with ideas for discussion in the Fitness Circles in the practice plans.

To give you more background information, we'll discuss some basics of health and fitness in this chapter. We'll begin with the components of fitness and continue with some general training principles and how they relate to fitness. We'll end this section by listing some healthy habits children should develop.

You also are responsible for the safety of your players while they are under your care, so we'll mention some specific precautions you can take. Because accidents may happen no matter how careful you are, though, we also list the steps you should take to prepare for injuries to players and describe some first aid procedures for minor injuries and heat illnesses. We conclude the chapter with a brief summary of the legal duties you must fulfill as a coach.

Components of Fitness

The main components of fitness you need to know about as a YMCA Rookies coach are these:

- Cardiorespiratory fitness
- Muscular strength and endurance
- Flexibility

Cardiorespiratory Fitness

As you might guess from the name, *cardiorespiratory fitness* is fitness of the heart (cardio) and circulatory system and the lungs (respiratory). It's also known as *aerobic fitness*. Training for cardiorespiratory fitness involves moving large muscle groups such as legs and arms in a rhythmic activity that is sustained for at least several minutes and uses large amounts of oxygen. Activities such as running, swimming, or bicycling are examples. Such training improves the transport of oxygen through the blood to working muscles by making the heart and lungs more efficient and the body better able to use the oxygen when it reaches the muscles. Someone who has cardiorespiratory fitness can engage in endurance activities without feeling winded or getting tired easily.

You can communicate some of the concepts related to cardiorespiratory fitness to young children. The following are some good examples:

- Physical activity (such as basketball) is good for fitness.
- The heart is a muscle that pumps our blood. Exercise makes it stronger.
- Our hearts beat faster when we exercise.

Encourage your players to be active at home, whether with basketball or other forms of physical activity.

Muscular Strength and Endurance

Muscles can be fit in two ways: They can be strong, and they can have endurance:

- *Strength* is the ability of a muscle to exert force against resistance, such as a weight. We use strength to perform everyday tasks, such as lifting a grocery bag or opening a door.
- *Endurance* is the ability of a muscle to exercise for an extended period of time without too much fatigue. It's useful in performing tasks that require repeated movements, such as vacuuming a carpet or washing a car.

Muscular strength and endurance can be improved with strength training, but, unless you have players who are so unusually weak that they have difficulty playing basketball, strength training is not necessary for children this age. Such training is more appropriate for older youth who want to train more seriously for the sport.

Your players will be able to understand these concepts related to muscular strength and endurance:

- We use arm and leg muscles when we play basketball.
- Playing basketball may strengthen leg muscles.
- Practicing dribbling strengthens arm muscles.

Flexibility

Flexibility involves the joints and muscles. It is the ability of the muscles around a joint to allow the joint its full range of motion. Being flexible makes movement easier.

For adults, stretching helps make muscles more flexible. Although it's not known if stretching is effective for children, we do advocate devoting a small amount of time to stretching before and after play. In this way, children learn the following proper techniques for stretching:

- Warm up with 5 to 10 minutes of low-intensity aerobic activity.
- Perform two repetitions of each stretch.
- Stretch to the point of a gentle pull, and then hold for 10 counts without bouncing.
- For cooling down, walk around to allow the heart and breathing rates to return to normal. Then perform three to five repetitions of each stretch before the muscles cool.

 ## Training Principles

You need to know just a few principles of training to work with players at this age level:

- The warm-up/cool-down principle
- The overload principle
- The reversibility principle
- The specificity principle

Warm-Up/Cool-Down Principle

Before beginning strenuous activity, players should perform some moderate warm-up activity that will increase body temperature, respiration, and heart rate and help prevent muscle and tendon strains and ligament sprains. Warm-up activities could be calisthenics, stretching, any games with small numbers of players, or skill drills that are not strenuous but include a lot of movement. Try to use warm-up activities that are interesting to your players.

After the strenuous activity is over, players should then slow down gradually with a cool-down activity. Stopping heavy activity abruptly can cause blood to pool in the legs and feet and can slow the removal of waste products created by muscle use. Light activity, such as walking or stretching, helps to keep blood circulating.

Overload Principle

Luckily for us, our bodies are very adaptable. We can present them with a workload a bit higher than what we've done before, and they will, over time, adapt to it. Each time our bodies adapt, we can then add more to what we've done before. This is how we can improve our fitness.

The body can be overloaded in three different ways:

- Increasing frequency by doing an activity more often
- Increasing intensity by putting more effort into an activity
- Increasing time by doing an activity longer

To remember these methods of overloading, think of the acronym FIT (frequency, intensity, and time). Increasing one or more of these aspects of activity or exercise will put a heavier load on the body. This principle can be used in all kinds of training. A weightlifter could add more weight as she grows stronger, adding intensity. A runner might add more miles or hours of training, adding time. Either one might choose to exercise more often during the week, increasing the frequency.

Overloading stimulates the body to make changes. Such changes involve the nervous system, which becomes able to recruit more muscle fibers; the circulation, which becomes better at distributing the blood to the working muscles; and the muscles, which produce new protein to meet working demands.

One caution about overloads—don't increase them too quickly, or you may cause injuries. A gradual approach is always safer.

Reversibility Principle

To state the reversibility principle briefly: Use it or lose it! Just as the body can make adaptations when given an overload, it can also lose its capabilities when it is not used. It takes three times as long to gain endurance as it does to lose it. If you stayed in bed for a week, you would lose nearly 10 percent of your aerobic fitness. Your strength would also decline, although not as fast. For this reason, you should encourage your players to be active both during and after the basketball season.

Specificity Principle

The specificity principle means that the type of training a person chooses to do should relate to his or her goal. For example, heavy weight training will not make a runner run faster. Bicycling will not improve swimming performance as much as additional swimming would. Performance improves most when the training done is specific to the desired activity.

Healthy Habits

One of the better things you can do for your players is to instill healthy habits. Being healthy is a lot easier when it becomes a routine part of life. Talk to your players about the benefits of being fit and eating well.

General Fitness

With all the distractions of video games and TV, many children are less active than they might otherwise be. Make a point of explaining to your players that being active will help them be healthier and feel better. It also may help their basketball game! Also discuss how other good health habits can help them, such as getting enough sleep, brushing their teeth and washing well, and saying no to tobacco, alcohol, and other drugs.

Good Nutrition

Good nutrition is not the first thing most young children think about when they choose foods. At this age, they may not even know which foods are good for them and which are not. You can start to make them aware of which foods will make them healthier and why good nutrition is important.

A simple guide for a good diet is the U.S. Department of Agriculture's food pyramid (see figure 10.1). This guide encourages us to eat lots of breads, cereals, rice, pasta, vegetables, and fruits; a smaller amount of meat, cheese, eggs, dried beans, or nuts; and only a very little bit of fats, oils, and sweets. Eating this way cuts down on the amount of fats in the diet and helps ensure an adequate amount of vitamins and minerals.

A serving of the foods in these groups is equal to the following:

- One-half cup of fruit or vegetable
- Three-fourths of a cup of juice
- One slice of bread
- One cup of milk
- One average piece of fruit
- One cup of salad greens
- One-half cup of cooked pasta
- Lean meat about the size of a deck of cards

According to Kalish (1996), the number of servings children should eat depends on their age, height, weight, and level of physical activity. One exception is milk; children need to have three milk group servings a day.

Safety Precautions

As a coach, you're morally and legally responsible for the safety of your players during practice sessions and games, so you need to take some regular

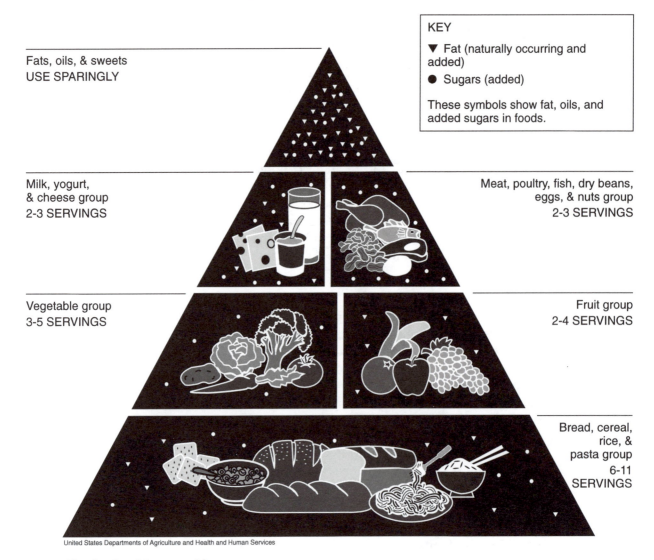

Figure 10.1 The food guide pyramid.

precautions to protect their safety. Some simple ways that you can protect your players from harm are requiring a preseason physical exam, regularly inspecting equipment and facilities, matching athletes by maturity, warning players and their parents of the potential for injury, supervising properly and keeping good records, and adjusting practices or games according to environmental conditions.

Preseason Physical Examination

We recommend that your players have a physical examination before participating in YMCA Rookies basketball. The exam should address the most likely areas of medical concern and identify youngsters at high risk. We also suggest that you have players' parents or guardians sign a participation agreement form and a release form to allow their children to be treated in case of an emergency. See appendix B, "Preparticipation Screening for YMCA Youth Sports Programs," for specific information on what should take place during the preseason physical examination.

Regular Inspection of Equipment and Facilities

Check the quality and fit of all of the protective equipment used by your players at the beginning of the season and inspect the equipment regularly during the season. Slick-soled, poor-fitting, or unlaced basketball shoes; unstrapped eyeglasses; and jewelry are dangerous on the basketball court—both to the player wearing such items and to other participants. Encourage players to switch into their basketball shoes when they reach playing sites so that the soles of their shoes are free of mud and moisture.

Remember, also, to examine regularly the court on which your players practice and play. Wipe up wet spots, remove hazards, report conditions you cannot remedy, and request maintenance as necessary. If unsafe conditions exist, either make adaptations to avoid risk to your players' safety or stop the practice or game until safe conditions have been restored.

Matching Athletes by Maturity

Children of the same age may differ in height and weight by up to 6 inches and 50 pounds. That's why, in contact sports or sports in which size provides an advantage, coaches must match players against opponents of similar size and physical maturity. Such an approach gives smaller, less physically mature children a better chance to succeed and avoid injury, and it provides larger children with more of a challenge.

Informing Players and Parents of Inherent Risks

You are legally responsible for warning players of the inherent risks involved in playing basketball. "Failure to warn" is one of the most successful arguments in lawsuits against coaches. You must thoroughly explain the inherent risks of basketball and make sure each player knows, understands, and appreciates those risks.

The preseason parent orientation meeting is a good opportunity to explain the risks of the sport to parents and players. It also is a good occasion on which to have both the players and their parents sign waivers releasing you from liability should an injury occur. Such waivers do not relieve you of responsibility for your players' well-being, but lawyers recommend them.

Proper Supervision and Record Keeping

With young children, simply being present in the area of play is not enough; you must actively plan and direct team activities and closely observe and evaluate players' participation. You're the watchdog responsible for the players' well-being, so if you notice a player limping or grimacing, give him or her a rest and examine the extent of the injury.

As part of your supervision duties, you are expected to foresee potentially dangerous situations and to help prevent them from occurring. As a coach, you're required to know and enforce the rules of the sport (especially safety rules), prohibit dangerous horseplay, and hold practice or games only under safe weather conditions (see the next section). These specific supervisory activities will make the play environment safer for your players and will help protect you from liability if a mishap does occur.

As a general rule, the more dangerous an activity is, the more closely you should be supervising players. This suggests that you need to directly supervise younger, less-experienced players, especially in riskier situations such as when they are learning new skills, are violating rules, or are tired or look unwell.

For further protection, keep records of your season plans, practice plans, and players' injuries. Season and practice plans come in handy when you need evidence that players have been taught certain skills, whereas accurate, detailed accident report forms offer protection against unfounded lawsuits. Ask for these forms from your YMCA and hold on to these records for several years so that an old basketball injury of a former player doesn't come back to haunt you.

Environmental Conditions

Although most basketball games may be played indoors, the following information is provided to inform coaches of the effects that environmental conditions can have, and to prepare them in the event that practice is held outdoors. Most problems due to environmental factors are related to excessive heat or cold, though you should also consider other environmental factors such as severe weather and pollution. Giving a little thought to potential problems and spending a little effort to ensure adequate protection for your players will prevent most serious emergencies related to environmental conditions.

Heat

On hot, humid days the body has difficulty cooling itself. Because the air is already saturated with water vapor (humidity), sweat doesn't evaporate as easily, and the body retains extra heat. Hot, humid environments make athletes prone to heat exhaustion and heatstroke (see more on these in "Providing First Aid" on pages 153–156). If you think it's hot or humid, it's worse on the kids, not just because they're more active, but because youngsters under the age of 12 have a more difficult time than adults regulating their body temperature.

To provide for players' safety in hot or humid conditions, take the following preventive measures:

◉ Monitor weather conditions and adjust practices or games accordingly. Figure 10.2 shows the specific air temperatures and humidity percentages that can be hazardous.

◉ Acclimatize players to exercising in high heat and humidity. Players can make adjustments to high heat and humidity over 7 to 10 days. During this time, hold practices at low to moderate activity levels and give the players water breaks every 20 minutes.

◉ Switch to light clothing. Players should wear shorts and white T-shirts.

◉ Identify and monitor players who are prone to heat illness. Those players who are overweight, heavily muscled, or out of shape will be more prone to heat illness, as will be those who work excessively hard or who have suffered heat illness before. Closely monitor these players and give them water breaks every 15 to 20 minutes.

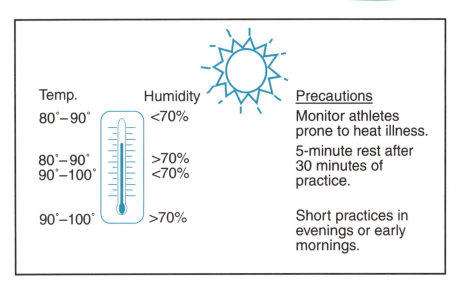

Figure 10.2 Air temperatures and humidity percentages.

◉ Make sure players replace water lost through sweat. Encourage your players to drink one liter of water each day, to drink eight ounces of water every 15 minutes during practice or games, and to drink four to eight ounces of water 15 minutes before practice or games.

◉ Replenish electrolytes lost through sweat, such as sodium (salt) and potassium. The best way to replace these nutrients is by eating a healthy diet that contains fresh fruits and vegetables. Bananas are a good source of potassium. The normal American diet contains plenty of salt, so players don't need to go overboard in salting their food to replace lost sodium.

Encourage players to drink plenty of water before, during, and after practice or games. Because water makes up 45 to 65 percent of a youngster's body weight, and water weighs about a pound per pint, the loss of even a little bit of water can have severe consequences for the body's systems. The weather doesn't have to be hot and humid for players to become dehydrated, nor do players have to feel thirsty. In fact, by the time they are aware of their thirst, they are long overdue for a drink.

Cold

When a person is exposed to cold weather, the body temperature starts to drop below normal. To counteract this drop, the body shivers and reduces the blood flow to gain or conserve heat. But no matter how effective the body's natural heating mechanism is, the body will better withstand cold temperatures if it is prepared to handle them. To reduce the risk of cold-related illnesses, make sure players wear appropriate protective clothing, and keep them active to maintain body heat. Also monitor the windchill (see figure 10.3 on page 150).

Severe Weather

Severe weather refers to a host of potential dangers, including lightning storms, the potential for tornadoes, hail, heavy rains (which can cause injuries by creating sloppy court conditions), and so on. Lightning is of special concern because it can come up quickly and can cause great harm or even kill. For

Windchill Index

Wind speed (mph) \ Temperature (°F)	0	5	10	15	20	25	30	35	40
40	-55	-45	-35	-30	-20	-15	-5	0	10
35	-50	-40	-35	-30	-20	-10	-5	5	10
30	-50	-40	-30	-25	-20	-10	0	5	10
25	-45	-35	-30	-20	-15	-5	0	10	15
20	-35	-30	-25	-15	-10	0	5	10	20
15	-30	-25	-20	-10	-5	0	10	15	25
10	-20	-15	-10	0	5	10	15	20	30
5	-5	0	5	10	15	20	25	30	35

Shaded region (wind 15–40 mph, temp 0–15°F and adjacent cells): Flesh may freeze within 1 minute.

Windchill temperature (°F)

Figure 10.3 Windchill index.

each five-second count from the flash of lightning to the bang of thunder, lightning is one mile away. A flash-bang of 10 seconds means lightning is two miles away; a flash-bang of 15 seconds indicates lightning is three miles away. You should stop a practice or competition for the day if lightning is three miles away or less (15 seconds or less from flash to bang).

Safe places in which to take cover when lightning strikes are fully enclosed metal vehicles with the windows up, enclosed buildings, and low ground (under cover of bushes, if possible). It's *not* safe to be near metallic objects, such as flag poles, fences, light poles, and metal bleachers. Also avoid trees, water, and open fields.

Cancel practice or a game when under either a tornado watch or warning. If for some reason you are playing when a tornado is nearby, you should get players inside a building, if possible. If not, have them lie in a ditch or low-lying area or crouch near a strong building, and use their arms to protect the head and neck.

The keys with severe weather are caution and prudence. Don't try to get that last 10 minutes of practice or a game in if lightning is on the horizon. Don't continue to play in heavy rains. Many storms can strike both quickly and ferociously. Respect the weather and play it safe.

Air Pollution

Poor air quality and smog can present real dangers to your players. Both short- and long-term lung damage are possible from participating in sports in unsafe air. Although participating in clean air is not possible in many areas, restricting activity is recommended when the air quality ratings are worse than moderate or when there is a smog alert. Your local health department or air-quality control board can inform you of the air-quality ratings for your area and whether they recommend restricting activities.

Emergency Care

No matter how good and thorough your prevention program, injuries may occur. When an injury does strike, chances are you will be the one in charge. The severity and nature of the injury will determine how actively involved you'll be in treating the injury, but regardless of how serious the injury is, you are responsible for knowing what steps to take. Let's look at how to prepare to provide basic emergency care to your injured players and how to take appropriate action when a minor injury or heat illness does occur.

Being Prepared

Being prepared to provide basic emergency care involves three steps: being trained in cardiopulmonary resuscitation (CPR) and first aid; having an appropriately stocked first aid kit on hand at practices or games; and having an emergency plan.

CPR and First Aid Training

We recommend that all YMCA Rookies coaches receive CPR and first aid training from a nationally recognized organization (the National Safety Council, the American Heart Association, the American Red Cross, or the American Sport Education Program, for example). You should be certified based on a practical and written test of knowledge. CPR training should include pediatric and adult basic life support and obstructed airway.

First Aid Kit

Be sure to have a first aid kit available at all practices and games. A well-stocked first aid kit should include the following:

- List of emergency phone numbers
- Change for a pay phone
- Face shield (for rescue breathing and CPR)
- Bandage scissors
- Plastic bags for crushed ice
- Three-inch and four-inch elastic wraps
- Triangular bandages
- Sterile gauze pads: three-inch and four-inch squares
- Saline solution for eyes
- Contact lens case
- Mirror
- Penlight
- Tongue depressors
- Cotton swabs
- Butterfly strips
- Bandage strips in assorted sizes
- Alcohol or peroxide
- Antibacterial soap
- First aid cream or antibacterial ointment
- Petroleum jelly
- Tape adherent and tape remover
- 1 1/2-inch white athletic tape
- Prewrap
- Sterile gauze rolls

- Insect sting kit
- Safety pins
- Eighth-inch, quarter-inch, and half-inch foam rubber
- Disposable surgical gloves
- Thermometer

Emergency Plan

An emergency plan is the final step in preparing to take appropriate action for severe or serious injuries. The plan calls for three steps:

1. Evaluate the injured player. Your CPR and first aid training will guide you here.

2. Call the appropriate medical personnel. If possible, delegate the responsibility of seeking medical help to another calm and responsible adult who is on hand for all practices and games. Write out a list of emergency phone numbers and keep it with you. Include the following phone numbers:

- Rescue unit
- Hospital
- Physician
- Police
- Fire department

Take each player's emergency information card to every practice and game (see appendix C). This information includes who to contact in case of an emergency, what types of medications the player is using, what types of drugs he or she is allergic to, and so on.

Give an emergency response card (see appendix D) to the contact person calling for emergency assistance. This card provides the information the contact person needs to convey and will help keep the person calm, knowing that everything he or she needs to communicate is on the card. Also complete an injury report form (see appendix E), and keep it on file for any injury that occurs.

3. Provide first aid. If medical personnel are not on hand at the time of the injury, you should provide first aid care to the extent of your qualifications. Although your CPR and first aid training will guide you here, the following are important notes:

- Do not move the injured player if the injury is to the head, neck, or back; if a large joint (ankle, knee, elbow, shoulder) is dislocated; or if the pelvis, a rib, or an arm or leg is fractured.
- Calm the injured player and keep others away from him or her as much as possible.
- Evaluate whether the player's breathing is stopped or irregular, and if necessary, clear the airway with your fingers.
- Administer artificial respiration if breathing has stopped. Administer CPR if the player's circulation has stopped.
- Remain with the player until medical personnel arrive.

Your emergency plan should follow this sequence:

1. Check the player's level of consciousness.
2. Send a contact person to call the appropriate medical personnel and to call the player's parents.
3. Send someone to wait for the rescue team and direct them to the injured player.
4. Assess the injury.
5. Administer first aid.
6. Assist emergency medical personnel in preparing the player for transportation to a medical facility.
7. Appoint someone to go with the player if the parents are not available. This person should be responsible, calm, and familiar with the player. Assistant coaches or parents are best for this job.
8. Complete an injury report form while the incident is fresh in your mind.

Providing First Aid

Proper CPR and first aid training, a well-stocked first aid kit, and an emergency plan help prepare you to take appropriate action when an injury occurs. In this section, we'll look at how to provide first aid both for minor injuries and for heat illnesses, which can be more serious. Keep in mind that some injuries are too severe for you to treat: head, neck, and back injuries; fractures; and injuries that cause a player to lose consciousness. In these cases, you should follow the emergency plan outlined on pages 152–153. Provide first aid *only to the extent of your qualifications*. Don't play doctor with injuries; sort out minor injuries that you can treat from situations in which you need to call for assistance.

Minor Injuries

Although no injury seems minor to the player who has it, most injuries are neither life-threatening nor severe enough to restrict participation. When such injuries occur, you can take an active role in their initial treatment. Most of the injuries you will see will be scrapes and cuts, strains and sprains, and bumps and bruises.

Scrapes and Cuts. When one of your players has an open wound, the first thing you should do is put on a pair of disposable surgical gloves or some other effective blood barrier. Don't let a fear of acquired immune deficiency syndrome (AIDS) stop you from helping a bleeding player. You are only at risk if you allow contaminated blood to come in contact with an open wound, so the blood barrier that you wear will protect you. Check with your director or the YMCA of the USA for more information about protecting yourself and your players from AIDS.

After you are wearing gloves, follow these four steps:

1. Stop the bleeding by applying direct pressure with a clean dressing to the wound and elevating it. The player may be able to apply this pressure

while you put on your gloves. Do not remove the dressing if it becomes soaked with blood. Instead, place an additional dressing on top of the one already in place. If bleeding continues, elevate the injured area above the heart and maintain pressure.

2. Cleanse the wound thoroughly once the bleeding is controlled. A good rinsing with a forceful stream of water, and perhaps light scrubbing with soap, will help prevent infection.

3. Protect the wound with sterile gauze or a bandage. If the player continues to participate, apply protective padding over the injured area.

4. Remove the gloves and dispose of them carefully to prevent you or anyone else from coming into contact with blood.

For bloody noses not associated with serious facial injury, have the athlete sit and lean slightly forward. Then pinch the player's nostrils shut. If the bleeding continues after several minutes, or if the player has a history of nosebleeds, seek medical assistance.

Strains and Sprains. The physical demands of playing basketball often result in injury to the muscles or tendons (strains) or to the ligaments (sprains). When your players suffer minor strains or sprains, immediately apply the PRICE method of injury care (see figure 10.4).

P Protect the player and injured body part from further danger or trauma.

R Rest the area to avoid further damage and foster healing.

I Ice the area to reduce swelling and pain.

C Compress the area by securing an ice bag in place with an elastic wrap.

E Elevate the injury above heart level to keep the blood from pooling in the area.

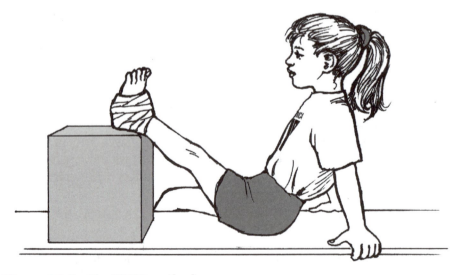

Figure 10.4   The PRICE method.

Bumps and Bruises. Inevitably, basketball players make contact with each other and with the court. If the force of a body part at impact is great enough, a bump or bruise will result. Many players continue playing with such sore spots, but if the bump or bruise is large and painful, you should act appropriately. Use the PRICE method of injury care and monitor the injury. If swelling, discoloration, and pain have lessened, the player may resume participation with protective padding; if not, a physician should examine the player.

Heat Illnesses

In case your team ever has to play under hot conditions, you also should know how to handle two types of heat illnesses: heat exhaustion and heatstroke.

Heat Exhaustion. Heat exhaustion is a shock-like condition caused by dehydration and electrolyte depletion. Symptoms include headache, nausea, dizziness, chills, fatigue, and extreme thirst (see figure 10.5 for heat exhaustion and heatstroke symptoms). Signs include pale, cool, and clammy skin; rapid, weak pulse; loss of coordination; dilated pupils; and profuse sweating (this is a key sign).

A player suffering from heat exhaustion should rest in a cool, shaded area; drink cool water; and have ice applied to the neck, back, or stomach to help cool the body. You may have to administer CPR if necessary or send for emergency medical assistance if the player doesn't recover or his or her condition worsens. Under no conditions should the player return to activity that day or before he or she regains all the weight lost through sweat. If the player had to see a physician, he or she shouldn't return to practice until released by the physician.

Heatstroke. Heatstroke is a life-threatening condition in which the body stops sweating and body temperature rises dangerously high. It occurs when dehydration causes a malfunction in the body's temperature control center in the brain. Symptoms include the feeling of being on fire (extremely hot), nausea, confusion, irritability, and fatigue. Signs include hot, dry, and flushed or red skin (this is a key sign); lack of sweat; rapid pulse; rapid breathing; constricted pupils; vomiting; diarrhea; and possibly seizures, unconsciousness, or respiratory or cardiac arrest. (See figure 10.5 for heat exhaustion and heatstroke symptoms.)

Send for emergency medical assistance immediately and have the player rest in a cool, shaded area. Remove excess clothing and equipment from the player, and cool his or her body with cool, wet towels or by pouring cool water over him or her. Apply ice packs to the armpits, neck, back, stomach, and between the legs. If the player is conscious, have him or her drink cool water. If the player is unconscious, place the player on his or her side to allow fluids and vomit to drain from the mouth. A player who has suffered heatstroke can't return to practice until he or she is released by a physician.

Legal Liability

When one of your players is injured, naturally your first concern is his or her well-being. Your concern for children, after all, is what made you decide to

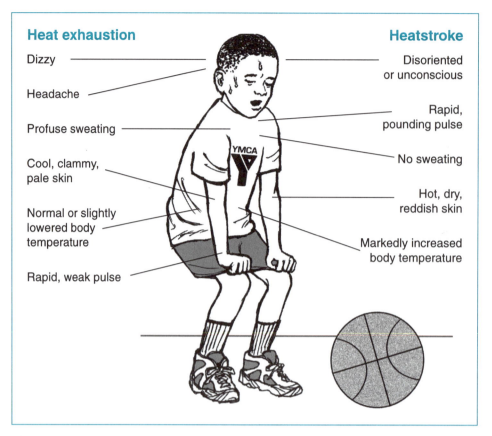

Figure 10.5 Symptoms of heat exhaustion and heatstroke.

coach. Unfortunately, you must also consider something else: Can you be held liable for the injury?

From a legal standpoint, a coach has nine duties to fulfill. In this chapter we've discussed all of them but planning (see chapters 5 through 7).

1. Provide a safe environment.
2. Properly plan the activity.
3. Provide adequate and proper equipment.
4. Match or equate athletes.
5. Warn of inherent risks in the sport.
6. Supervise the activity closely.
7. Evaluate athletes for injury or incapacitation.
8. Know emergency procedures and first aid.
9. Keep adequate records.

In addition to fulfilling these nine legal duties, you should check your YMCA's insurance coverage and your own personal coverage to make sure you are protected from liability.

chapter 11

Teaching Character Development

This final chapter will deal with character development, the teaching of values to players. At the YMCA, teaching values is as important a part of the basketball program as teaching game skills. As a YMCA coach, you take on the responsibility to help children learn about and use four core values that the YMCA has chosen to emphasize: caring, honesty, respect, and responsibility.

You can teach these values in several ways:

- Communicate to your players that sporting behavior is an important part of the program.
- Teach the four values to players so they know what those values mean. Give them examples.
- Include the values in each practice session (character development discussions appear in each practice plan).
- Consistently model those values in your own behavior so players can see what those values look like.
- Celebrate those values and hold them up to players as what is right in order to help them learn to believe in the values.
- Ask players to practice the values over and over again.
- Consistently reinforce and reward behaviors that support the values, using the specific value word that is relevant: "Cindy, thanks for helping Kolicia find the ball. That shows caring."

- Consistently confront a player whose behavior is inconsistent with the values, but do so in a way that does not devalue him or her.
- Be prepared to talk to parents about the character development portion of the basketball program.

Teaching values involves a somewhat different approach than teaching skills:

- First, it requires you to be a good role model. You should set an example with your words and actions.
- Second, you need to understand at what level your players are capable of understanding and applying values. Younger children do not think about moral decisions in the same way as adults. Children gradually develop the ability to understand values as they grow.
- Third, you need to learn to identify situations during practice that relate to the four values. Many everyday occurrences provide a chance for you to demonstrate to players that values are relevant to their daily lives.
- Finally, you can use the Team Circle discussions suggested in the practice plans or find activities of your own, ones that emphasize values and make players think about them.

Being a Good Role Model

Most of us believe in the YMCA's core values of caring, honesty, respect, and responsibility, but we don't always follow our own beliefs. Our character is measured by our behavior. We judge ourselves by our good intentions. Other people judge us only by our behavior. Consider the following lists of coaching behaviors for each value. These lists aren't meant to be comprehensive; they're meant to get you thinking about what being a good role model means, in practical terms, as it applies to these four important values.

Caring

- You spend time after practice helping a player learn a skill.
- You comfort a player who is dejected after a loss.
- You help a player who is stressed manage that stress.
- You inform your players of the benefits of good nutrition.

Honesty

- You tell a player that she's not executing a skill correctly and you'll help her.
- You tell a player when you don't know a rule (but you'll find out).
- You tell a player when you make a mistake, such as misinterpreting who instigated minor misbehavior during practice.

- You tell your team that you haven't been as physically active in the off-season as you'd like to be, but you're trying to improve.

Respect

- You don't blow your cool when players misbehave.
- You listen to players attentively when they are talking.
- You bring the same energy and enthusiasm for teaching skills to all your players, no matter how skilled they are.
- You don't criticize players in front of their teammates.

Responsibility

- You show up on time and prepared for all practices and contests.
- You provide appropriate first aid for injured players.
- You supervise all practice activities closely.
- You intervene when players are misbehaving.

Understanding Children's Moral Reasoning

As you work with children on character development, you need to keep in mind how they think about moral questions. They approach such questions much differently than an adult would, and their perspective changes as they grow. One researcher, Kohlberg (Bee 1995; Crain 1992), has developed a set of stages for thinking about moral questions that he believes children move through as they mature.

Children up through the age of nine generally think about moral questions in terms of obedience and punishment. They assume that fixed rules are set by powerful adults who can enforce those rules by punishment. Children are doing right when they obey the rules unquestioningly. Actions are judged by their outcomes, not by the person's intentions. Moral reasoning for children nine and younger is very black-and-white. In basketball, you might expect to see children interpret an opponent's personal foul as an intentional attack when it is most likely unintentional and a result of poor skill or lack of experience.

Around the age of 10, most children think about moral questions in terms of what works best for them. The right thing is the thing that brings pleasant results. They also think about making deals with others—if I do something for you, then you may, in turn, do something for me. Making fair deals is important. A 10- or 11-year-old may agree to congratulate the opponent on good plays or at the end of a game because he or she knows that the behavior pleases most adults and most other children. If the opponent doesn't congratulate his or her good play in return, however, he or she may stop that behavior because it doesn't generate a pleasant or fair result.

Near 16, most players have started thinking about moral questions in terms of how those questions relate to the expectations of their family and community. The key focus is behaving in good ways and having good motives and good feelings toward others. At this point, players also start to take into account people's intentions when judging actions.

These players can better understand their roles as representatives of their team or their YMCA and as role models for younger players, particularly when their coaches, parents, and teammates encourage them. Such encouragement would be likely to cause them to modify their game behaviors to fulfill others' expectations.

Moving from one type of thinking about morality to another happens gradually and may occur at different ages for different children. This outline gives you some broad guidelines for how the majority of the players on your team may look at character development questions when you bring them up in Team Circles or during practice or games.

Using Teachable Moments

During practices, you may find that a situation arises that gives you a chance to point out how values apply. This type of situation is known as a *teachable moment*, and it might be something like one team's behavior toward an opponent, one player's behavior toward another, or a violation of team rules. Use teachable moments when they occur. Stop a skill practice or game to comment on an incident. Don't do this too frequently, but using this approach can be effective when a good opportunity arises to illustrate a value discussed earlier.

A teachable moment can be triggered by either good or bad actions; you can praise an individual's or group's supportive, fair behavior or stop an activity briefly to talk about negative behavior. Try to balance positive and negative instances; don't use just negative situations. Here are some examples:

- If one player yells at another for a mistake in play, talk to that player about respect.
- If a player does something dangerous during a game, have a brief discussion with that player about responsibility and caring for others.
- If a player helps another child who is hurt, praise the player for being caring.
- If a player raises her hand to admit committing a foul that wasn't called, congratulate that player for being honest.

Teachable moments are occasions on which you can hold up the right value and explain why it is the acceptable thing to do. Doing this illustrates to players what values look like beyond the words and how values are a part of our everyday lives.

Using Values Activities

Each practice plan includes a Team Circle, which gives you a topic for brief discussion of one or more of the core values. Just as practice drills focus on physical skills, Team Circles focus on character development. They help players realize that participation in basketball also teaches them about themselves and others.

Try using these tips when leading Team Circle discussions:

- Begin discussions by reviewing the YMCA House Rules: speak for yourself, listen to others, avoid put-downs, take charge of yourself, and show respect. (Repeat these rules in your first three or four Team Circles; after that, you'll probably only need to reinforce these House Rules occasionally.)

- Be yourself. Children respect an adult who listens to them and who talks honestly.

- As a role model for your players, be willing to admit mistakes; it will make players more likely to be open about themselves.

- Give players a chance to respond, but allow them to pass if they want to. Reinforce their responses with a nod, smile, or short comment like "Thanks," "Okay," "That's interesting," or "I understand." Give the player speaking your undivided attention.

- After all players have had a chance to respond to your Team Circle question, briefly summarize the responses and add your own comments. Try not to lecture.

You might also include activities of your own that reinforce values. The YMCA of the USA has created a number of character development resources; ask your YMCA if they can make those available to you. These ideas were taken from the YMCA Character Development Activity Box (YMCA of the USA, 1997):

- Tell your players that one way to demonstrate caring is to do kind things for others. Ask the players to brainstorm ideas of things they could do to be kind to the other members of their families. Some ideas might be washing dishes, cleaning their rooms, or telling a story to a younger brother or sister. Encourage each player to do one kind act for each member of his or her family during the next week, and discuss what they did during the next week's practice.

- Point out that on a team, all players must respect their teammates, because they are not a team without every one of them. Divide the team into two equal groups. Have each group line up in single file as fast as they can in the order you tell them to. They can race to see which group can line up the fastest.

First, say, "I want you to line up from shortest to tallest." After both groups have done that, indicate who won and congratulate both groups. Then say, "Now line up by birthday month, with January in the front and December in the back." Next, say, "Line up by biggest foot to smallest." Finish by saying, "Okay, everybody have a seat back in the circle."

Ask, "Now, in that game, who were the most important players: the short ones or the tall ones? That's right, all were equally important. The same is true for when you were born or how big your foot is. The fact is that every person is important on a team and worthy of your respect. Teamwork is when everyone does his or her part, no matter what that is or how much attention it gets."

◎ Discuss with your players the idea of cooperation versus competition. Point out that the other team makes the game possible. Ask the players to brainstorm ways they might show respect to the other team. These might include saying positive things to the opposing players, congratulating them for outstanding plays, and shaking hands at the end of a game. Encourage your players to do these things when they play.

Any activities you use should meet these criteria:

- ◎ Be age-appropriate and developmentally appropriate.
- ◎ Account for varied personal backgrounds and differing views on values.
- ◎ Attempt to change players' attitudes as well as actions.
- ◎ Focus on long-term results.
- ◎ Be planned and intentional.
- ◎ Fit logically with what you are doing.
- ◎ Be positive and constructive, not putting players down.
- ◎ Be inclusive.
- ◎ Be meaningful, not trivial or corny.
- ◎ Be fun!

Appendix A

Finding More Information

 **Books**

Garchow, Karen, and Amy Dickinson. 1992. *Youth Basketball: A Complete Handbook*. Dubuque, IA: Brown and Benchmark.

> Four individual guides that cover topics such as rules, skills and drills, offensive and defensive strategies, working with parents, motivating players, preventing injury, and conditioning.

Williams, Joe, and Stan Wilson. 1993. *Youth League Basketball*. Indianapolis: Masters Press.

> Coaches of beginning players will be able to use this collection of offense and defense drills and coaching tips. It also covers injury prevention, morale, and practice procedures.

Wissel, Hal. 1994. *Basketball: Steps to Success*. Champaign, IL: Human Kinetics.

> A step-by-step approach to learning basketball skills for teens and adults. It includes 113 drills for improving offensive and defensive skills.

 **Videos**

American Sport Education Program. 1994. *Teaching Youth Basketball Basics*. Champaign, IL: Human Kinetics.

> This video shows how coaches can use the IDEA method for teaching basic skills (the method used in YMCA Youth Super Sports). It covers the fundamentals of shooting, dribbling, rebounding, and setting and defending screens.

Wooden, John. *Teaching Kids Basketball.* ESPN Home Video.

> Wooden, UCLA's most successful coach, shows kids how to pass, dribble, shoot, rebound, and defend. The video includes segments on injury prevention and conditioning, as well as drills.

 Organizations

USA Basketball
5465 Mark Dabling Blvd.
Colorado Springs, CO 80918-3842
Phone: 719-590-4800

Youth Basketball of America
P. O. Box 3067
Orlando, FL 32802-8201
Phone: 407-363-YBOA

Appendix B

Preparticipation Screening for YMCA Youth Sports Programs

 ## A Statement of the YMCA of the USA Medical Advisory Committee

The YMCA believes in providing a safe experience for all youth participating in YMCA sports programs. Although staff and other program leaders are primarily responsible for the health and safety of the child during training and competition, it is equally important for parents to determine that their children participating in YMCA sports have no medical conditions that would preclude their participation or result in further injury or harm.

The YMCA of the USA Medical Advisory Committee recommends that YMCAs encourage parents of youth participating in YMCA sports programs to have their children screened for the purpose of: (1) determining the general health of the child; (2) detecting medical or musculoskeletal conditions that may predispose a child to injury or illness during competition; and (3) detecting potentially life-threatening or disabling conditions that may limit a child's participation.

Appendix B

The following 10 questions are particularly important for a physician to ask during a sports pre-participation exam (*Preparticipation Physical Evaluation* 1997):

1. Have you ever passed out during or after exercise?
2. Have you ever been dizzy during or after exercise?
3. Have you ever had chest pain during or after exercise?
4. Do you get tired more quickly than your friends do during exercise?
5. Has your heart ever raced or skipped heartbeats?
6. Have you ever had high blood pressure or high cholesterol?
7. Have you ever been told you have a heart murmur?
8. Has any family member or relative died of heart problems or a sudden death before age 50?
9. Have you had a severe viral infection (for example, myocarditis or mononucleosis) within the last month?
10. Has a physician ever denied or restricted your participation in sports for any heart problems?

Although this list is not complete, these questions address the most likely areas of concern and are the most helpful in identifying individuals at high risk. A "yes" answer to any of these questions should result in further evaluation and a discussion between physician and parent about appropriate sports participation for the child.

On the registration form for each youth sports program, there should be a statement requiring a parent's/guardian's signature that indicates that the child has been properly screened and that there are no medical conditions or injuries that preclude his or her participation in that sport.

Preparticipation Physical Evaluation, Second Edition, American Academy of Family Physicians, American Academy of Pediatrics, American Medical Society for Sports Medicine, American Orthopaedic Society for Sports Medicine, American Osteopathic Academy of Sports Medicine, 1997.

Appendix C

Emergency Information Card

Athlete's name _____ Age _____
Address _____
Phone _____ S.S.# _____
Sport _____

List two persons to contact in case of emergency:

Parent or guardian's name _____ Home phone _____
Address _____ Work phone _____

Second person's name _____ Home phone _____
Address _____ Work phone _____
Relationship to athlete

Insurance co. _____ Policy # _____
Physician's name _____ Phone _____

IMPORTANT

Is your child allergic to any drugs? _____ If so, what? _____
Does your child have any other allergies? (e.g., bee stings, dust) _____
Does your child suffer from ____ asthma, ____ diabetes, or ____ epilepsy? (Check any that apply.)
Is your child on any medication? _____ If so, what? _____

Does your child wear contacts? _____

Is there anything else we should know about your child's health or physical condition? If yes, please explain. _____
_____
_____
_____
_____

Signature _____ Date _____

Appendix D

Emergency Response Card

Information for Emergency Call (be prepared to give this information to the EMS dispatcher)

1. Location _____
   Street address _____
   City or town _____
   Directions (cross streets, landmarks, etc.) _____
   _____

2. Telephone number from which the call is being made _____

3. Caller's name _____

4. What happened _____
   _____
   _____
   _____
   _____
   _____

5. How many persons injured _____

6. Condition of victim(s) _____

7. Help (first aid) being given _____

Note: Do not hang up first. Let the EMS dispatcher hang up first.

Appendix E

Injury Report

Name of athlete _____

Date _____

Time _____

First aider (name) _____

Cause of injury _____

Type of injury _____

Anatomical area involved _____

Extent of injury _____

First aid administered _____

Other treatment administered _____
_____

Referral action _____
_____

_____
First aider (signature)

Resources and Suggested Readings

American Academy of Family Physicians, American Academy of Pediatrics, American Medical Society for Sports Medicine, American Orthopaedic Society for Sports Medicine, American Osteopathic Academy of Sports Medicine. 1997. *Preparticipation physical evaluation, second edition.*

American Sport Education Program. 1996. *Coaching youth basketball* (2nd ed.). Champaign, IL: Human Kinetics.

Bee, Helen. 1995. *The developing child* (7th ed.). New York: HarperCollins College.

Berk, Laura E. 1998. *Development through the lifespan.* Needham Heights, MA: Allyn & Bacon.

Crain, William. 1992. *Theories of development: Concepts and applications* (3rd ed.). Englewood Cliffs, NJ: Prentice Hall.

Flegel, Melinda J. 1997. *Sport first aid* (Updated Edition). Champaign, IL: Human Kinetics.

Golding, Lawrence A., Clayton R. Myers, and Wayne E. Sinning. 1989. *Y's way to physical fitness* (3rd ed.). Champaign, IL: Human Kinetics.

Humphrey, James H. 1993. *Sports for children: A guide for adults.* Springfield, IL: Charles C Thomas.

Kalish, Susan. 1996. *Your child's fitness: Practical advice for parents.* Champaign, IL: Human Kinetics.

Martens, Rainer, and Robert W. Christina, John S. Harvey, Jr., and Brian J. Sharkey. 1981. *Coaching young athletes.* Champaign, IL: Human Kinetics.

YMCA of the USA. 1990. *YMCA Youth fitness program.* Champaign, IL: Human Kinetics.

YMCA of the USA. 1997. *Character development activity box.* Chicago: YMCA of the USA.